Recently a radio ... lyn, what is your definit

I was surprised ... nough I have written two books abou ... have been interviewed many times on t... ject, no one had ever asked me for a definition. I whispered a quick prayer, *Lord, please give me a helpful and concise answer.*

"Grief is the process of facing the death of a dream," I answered.

The interviewer took a deep breath and said, "Oh, I like that. I've had many dreams die."

*   *   *

Marilyn Heavilin offers you hope and encouragement in the face of your dream that has died. Through a process of

- **Letting Go** . . . of grief, unforgiveness and shattered dreams

- **Launching Out** . . . spiritually, emotionally, in truth, in prayer

- **Living Again** . . . with confidence, even when your dreams have died

you'll discover how she — and others who experienced the death of their dreams — learned to begin again.

Also by Marilyn Willett Heavilin

Roses in December: Finding Strength Within Grief

December's Song: Handling the Realities of Grief

Mother to Daughter: Becoming a Woman of Honor

MARILYN WILLETT HEAVILIN

When your Dreams Die

Here's Life Publishers

First Printing, June 1990
Second Printing, October 1990

Published by
HERE'S LIFE PUBLISHERS, INC.
P. O. Box 1576
San Bernardino, CA 92402

Cover design by Cornerstone Graphics

Library of Congress Cataloging-in-Publication Data
Heavilin, Marilyn Willett.
When your dreams die : finding strength and hope through life's disappoint-
ments / Marilyn Willett Heavilin.
p.   cm.
Includes bibliographical references.
ISBN 0-89840-268-9
1. Christian life — 1960- . 2. Consolation. I. Title.
BV4501.2.H3694   1990
248.8'6 — dc 20   90-33883
                                  CIP

For More Information, Write:
L.I.F.E. — P.O. Box A399, Sydney South 2000, Australia
Campus Crusade for Christ of Canada — Box 300, Vancouver, B.C., V6C 2X3, Canada
Campus Crusade for Christ — Pearl Assurance House, 4 Temple Row, Birmingham, B2 5HG, England
Lay Institute for Evangelism — P.O. Box 8786, Auckland 3, New Zealand
Campus Crusade for Christ — P.O. Box 240, Raffles City Post Office, Singapore 9117
Great Commission Movement of Nigeria — P.O. Box 500, Jos, Plateau State Nigeria, West Africa
Campus Crusade for Christ International — Arrowhead Springs, San Bernardino, CA 92414, U.S.A.

To those who have watched dreams die—
May you be encouraged to dream again.

Contents

.

Letting Go

Broken Dreams

As children bring their broken
toys with tears for us to mend,
I brought my broken dreams to God
because He was my Friend.

But then instead of leaving Him
in peace to work alone,
I hung around and tried to help
with ways that were my own.

At last I snatched them back and
cried, "How can you be so slow?"
"My child," He said, "What could I do?
You never did let go."

          —Author unknown[1]

1

Letting Go
of Your Grief

I was hurrying to get ready for a Tuesday morning Bible study. The television was on, but I wasn't paying much attention to it until the announcer said, "Ladies and Gentlemen, there has been a problem with the launching of the *Challenger*." They replayed the brief film that was available. The *Challenger* took to the sky just as other shuttles had done in the past. Then something went wrong and the *Challenger* exploded into flames. All of us who watched knew in our hearts what had happened—but no one wanted to believe it was true.

Before the families of the crew members were rushed away, a few cameramen caught the horror-stricken look on their faces—that look of panic, disbelief and grief all wrapped into one. The world wept in unison. We had experienced the death of a dream and we grieved together.

When we hear the word *grief*, our minds immediately think of physical death. But just as our country grieved not only for the deaths of the *Challenger* crew but also for the failure of the space program, I have discovered that we, too, grieve over all kinds of losses and changes in our lives.

The Death of a Dream

Recently a radio interviewer asked me, "Marilyn, what is your definition of grief?"

I was surprised by his question. Although I have written two books about grief and have been interviewed many times on the subject, no one had ever asked me for a definition. I whispered a quick prayer, *Lord, please give me a helpful and concise answer.*

"Grief is the process of facing the death of a dream," I answered.

The interviewer took a deep breath and said, "Oh, I like that. I've had many dreams die." God had answered my prayer.

Melody Beattie, author of *Codependent No More,* writes:

> Perhaps the most painful loss many codependents face is the loss of our dreams, the hopeful and sometimes idealistic expectations for the future that most people have. This loss can be the most difficult to accept. As we looked at our child in the hospital nursery, we had certain hopes for him or her. Those hopes didn't include our child having a problem with alcohol or other drugs. Our dreams didn't include this. On our wedding day, we had dreams. The future with our beloved was full of wonder and promise. This was the start of something great, something loving, something we had long hoped for. The dreams and promises may have been spoken or unspoken but for most of us, they were there.[2]

Through the past year, I've shared my definition of grief with hundreds of people and have consistently received a positive reaction. In fact, people frequently have volunteered the stories of their own dreams that have died. Often, though, in these people I sense that the process of grieving has not been completed.

Our society is so anxious for us to "get over it" and return "back to normal" that we are often deprived of the healing brought by grieving: facing the hurt, growing stronger as we struggle with the changes brought about in our lives when our dreams die, deciphering what all of this grief and pain says about us and means to us. Unless we go through this process, many potentially significant opportunities for growth in our lives are missed because we stuff our pain away, put on a happy face, and say, "I'm just fine." This kind of denial will lead us into situations where we make unwise and hurried decisions which we often regret later.

I have seen many who are recovering from the death of a spouse or a divorce decide to rid themselves of all reminders of their past life immediately. In the case of divorce, a spouse may go so far as to cut the former spouse out of all the family pictures or burn all the pictures that person was in. Such extreme actions may temporarily help the individual but those same actions can be devastating to other members of the family whose grief is moving at a slower and more natural rate.

I have talked to many children of divorce who have suffered a great deal of additional pain because their parents' anger at each other spilled over on them. Parents who refuse to talk about the estranged parent are doing a great disservice to their children. Often the children feel they have no roots, or if the estranged parent was so bad that no one will talk about him or her, then they as children of that person must be bad as well.

I recently heard a counselor state on the radio, "It should be our objective to resolve our pain and then give it a proper burial. But most of us bury our pain alive without any resolution and then wonder why the pain keeps trying to resurrect."

I have had several dreams die — some big, some small, but they all mattered to me. The most poignant deaths of dreams were the deaths of three of my children. Our family's story is told in my books *Roses in December* and *December's Song.*

Bad Things Can Happen to Good People

Our third child, Jimmy, died of crib death when he was seven weeks old. At Jimmy's death, the first dream I buried was the dream that we would live happily ever after in a lovely home with healthy, wonderful children. I hadn't left any room in that dream for problems — at least not problems such as the death of a child. I believed bad things wouldn't happen to good people. Jimmy's death didn't fit into my dream of a perfect, trouble-free life. But I didn't want to let go of that dream. I thought everything would go according to my plan from then on.

A year and a half later, when our identical twins, Nathan and Ethan, were born, it was so easy for me to think God was trying to pay me back for the child who had died — a sort of peace offering. And to make it even more unique, those children were born on Christmas morning. What a special, special Christmas present.

Ten days later we were told Ethan had pneumonia and the doctors did not expect him to live. As my husband Glen and I sat in the hospital that night, I remember struggling with my pain and thinking, *God, this isn't fair. How can you do this? I thought you called me to be a mother, and I was doing a good job at it. Now you are taking another child away.*

Ethan's death destroyed my dream that people who experience a major trauma will be exempt from any further cataclysmic events. I was vulnerable. It could happen again — even if I was a good person. And I watched the dream of raising identical twins die right before my eyes.

We then lived seventeen years without any major traumas in our immediate family. Matthew, our oldest son, Mellyn, our only daughter, and Nathan, the remaining twin, developed into beautiful young people. I allowed myself to feel safe and secure. I dreamed dreams of Nathan's high school and college graduations, our children's weddings, and our children's and grandchildren's presence in our family for the rest of my life. I dreamed that my three remaining children would live successful lives, have happy families, serve God and, most of all, outlive me. I still could not let go of my dream of everything going my way.

I thought I had life all put together. When I was twenty, I had quit college after two years to marry my husband. For many years after that I spent my time raising children. When my two oldest were in high school, I thought it was time for mom to go back to college. Even though I didn't show a lot of ability when I was in college the first time, I knew it would be different now. I had raised my kids. I had time to concentrate on myself. And I had the major questions of life settled (Am I going to marry? Who am I going to marry? When am I going to marry?).

I started college again when I was thirty-nine and I earned my degree in about four years. I majored in Liberal Studies and began working on a masters in Counselor Education to prepare me to be a high school academic counselor. My first position was in the high school where my son Nathan was a sophomore. It was fun to be with him.

When my other kids were in high school I was able to be with them as a lay reader in their high school. It was an unusual position; no one else had ever had the position in that high school, but I believe God created it for me. I was able to talk with young people and help them with learning disabilities. I really enjoyed occasionally having lunch with Matt and Mellyn, being able to know what they were doing, and also keeping in touch with their friends.

My first year on the job at Nathan's high school was exciting. The school was only a year and a half old when I started working there. Since this was Nate's first time to attend a private school, he and I pioneered together in our endeavors and really had a good time.

Then on February 10, 1983, Nathan was on the way home from a high school basketball game when a drunk driver crossed the center line and hit Nathan's car head on at sixty-five miles per hour. Nathan lived long enough to arrive at the hospital and for us to get there, but after three hours we were once again hearing the words, "I'm sorry, but your child is dead."

Many of my dreams for my family died with Jimmy and Ethan. But the death of Nathan affected me in ways that reached beyond my family.

At work I had enjoyed so much being with the young people because I had kids their age. And one of the things which had drawn me to that particular school was the opportunity to be with my own son. Suddenly all of that changed.

After Nate's death, I found the rides to and from work, which I had once looked forward to, were now a nightmare. Those twelve-mile drives from San Bernardino to Redlands and back used to be fun and exciting when I could talk to Nate and his friends. I didn't enjoy being alone. I also had to drive near the spot where Nathan had been killed, and I frequently went by the wrecking yard where his crumpled car remained for several weeks. By the time I got to school every morning, even if I had left home in a good mood, I was a mess. And I was often in tears when I arrived home in the afternoon.

I spent much time on my job counseling many of Nate's friends — those kids who had plans of going to college with my Nate, those who had competed with him to get the highest score on the PSAT, the ones who wanted to be the best in their math class or get the most points in the basketball game. Now Nate wasn't there and my whole outlook about my job changed. I remained at the school for two years, but I did not enjoy it. I realized God was allowing another dream to die, a dream I had prepared for, a dream I really thought was going to come true. I had my degree. I almost had my credential. I was ready to do this work. But the love was gone. The desire was gone. My vocational dream was slipping away.

I had known Nathan would go off to college someday. Glen and I were looking forward to the time we would have alone. But we expected we would have more time to prepare for the empty nest. We looked forward to helping Nate choose a school, talking about the girls he was dating, and watching him mature. Another dream gone. What could I do now?

Not Exactly as You Planned

I'm sure all of you have watched your plans get altered in some way. Perhaps some of your changes are normal, natural processes, but they are still difficult. You may have had the opportunity to watch your children grow up, go to college, get married and establish their own homes, but you still find yourself grieving for the life that used to be. Don't be hard on yourself. It's all right to grieve over these changes. We need to give ourselves time to move from old dreams to new dreams.

Some changes, though, may not have been a part of your original plan. Perhaps you've been catapulted into a divorce you didn't want . . . a child has walked away from you . . . a family member has died. Perhaps there have been financial changes which require decisions you didn't plan on making. You may be experiencing physical changes. You may have been a very healthy person, and now the body that you depended on is disabled in some way.

My friend Helen writes:

> I had just turned forty years old, and I seemed to "have it all." My "all" included a good education with a graduate degree; a profession in which I excelled and was recognized by my peers; a wonderful husband; two healthy, happy, bright children; and a lovely home. My dreams had come true.
>
> As a child, I dreamed of becoming a musician and teacher. My family discouraged me, not out of malice but to spare me what they thought would be inevitable disappointment. A few of my relatives in my parents' generation (first generation children of immigrants) had finished high school, but most had dropped out at an early age to go to work to help support the family. No one on either side of the family had attended college. Since we had a small farm that barely supported us, there was no extra money for education. I was not discouraged, however, because I had a *plan* and was determined to make my dreams come true. I would pay my own way and, with the help of scholarships, I would earn a college degree and play and teach beautiful music.
>
> For twenty years, nothing did stop me. Of course there were setbacks and hard times along the way, but life was wonderful because I was doing what I loved best. Of course, I thanked God for my good fortune and donated much of my time and talent to the work of our church. But I still felt very much in control of my earthly destiny.
>
> Then one night a peculiar thing happened. I was taking an evening university course and when I got up after sitting through a three-hour lecture, I noticed I had some numbness in my lower right leg. It was still there

the next morning. During the next couple of weeks the numbness spread, so I went to the doctor. Over the course of the next few months I went through the frustrating experience of being sent from doctor to doctor, specialist to specialist, none of whom could pin down what was wrong. By this time I was completely numb from the waist down, was having muscle spasms in my chest, had little control over bodily eliminations, and began to fall down occasionally. Finally, I was diagnosed with multiple sclerosis.

Since standing and doing musical conducting was now physically impossible for me, my school district agreed to transfer me to a regular classroom to teach math. I prayed for remission. Instead, I got weaker and fell down several times at school, the last time requiring a trip to the emergency room to patch me up. That did it. The school district would no longer take responsibility for my safety and I had to begin proceedings to take disability retirement.

Helen's doctor told her that the course of MS is unpredictable. A full or partial remission was always possible, but if her condition continued to decline at the present rate, she would soon be in a wheelchair and her life expectancy might be as little as three years.

Helen told me she felt a great deal of anger toward God. How could He do this to her? Didn't He know that she had worked and planned all her life to get where she was? Didn't He know that she couldn't stand the possibility of not seeing her children grow up? And what about her husband—how was he going to cope? Didn't God remember that she'd gone to church regurlarly and donated a lot of her time and talent to His service? It just wasn't fair.

Perhaps your broken dream is a damaged childhood. Your parents did not know how to love you as they should. You may have been abused sexually, emotionally or physically—betrayed by someone you trusted.

Marion West states, "Grief is to healing what labor is to a delivery. To prevent it or even slow it down would be unnatural, disastrous. Grief is really our unsuspected friend who introduces us to healing."[3]

How about you? Are you grieving over a dream that has died, been altered or broken? Where do you feel you are in that process right now?

Early Stages of Grief

Most of us who have grieved are probably familiar with the stages of grief as described by Elizabeth Kubler Ross in her book *On Death and Dying*. Since Dr. Ross's "stages" are feelings or emotions, for the sake of clarity and understanding I would prefer to call her stages "responses" to grief. These "responses" do not necessarily come in order and you may experience several emotions at one time or repeatedly.

The stages I refer to in this book are progressional. One stage will follow the other, and once you have moved to the next stage you will probably not go back unless a new trauma occurs.

In the early stages of grief, it is not uncommon to spend a lot of time thinking about heaven. What do they do there? Are they aware of us? Do they know what we are doing? Many people begin to long for the second coming of Christ because this world is too painful.

You may feel completely hopeless. The thought that your pain will ever subside probably seems impossible. The idea that you will ever enjoy life again seems ludicrous. Holidays, birthdays, death days and anniversaries will seem intolerable, and your goal will be simply to endure and live through them.

You may feel disoriented, removed from what's going on around you, numb to feelings or emotions. In the early stages of grief, it is not unusual for people to have little desire to live. Six months after Nathan's death I contracted pneumonia, and I didn't have the strength to fight. It truly didn't matter to me whether I lived or died.

You may experience deep or mild depression and feel that no one understands your pain. You may vacillate between incessant talking and total silence. Most early grievers are oblivious to anyone else's pain and don't want to know that others are hurting.

Middle Stages of Grief

In the middle stages of grief, the pain will subside every once in a while for at least brief moments. Some days your grief will not be your waking thought, although you will still think about it frequently through the day. Waves of grief still come, but they will not last as long or come as often. You may begin to realize that others have problems which seem even more difficult than yours, and you may occasionally find yourself offering help and advice to another hurting person.

Holidays will not be dreaded quite so much, but you have probably learned by now you don't have to be tied to traditions ("We've *always* done it this way"). You will feel the freedom to celebrate special occasions in your own style. Death days, birthdays and anniversaries will still probably be quite uncomfortable.

In the middle stages of grief, as you become more fully aware of the injustice of your situation, you may become obsessed with the thought that you must change the wrongs of the world. Grieving people can become driven and single-minded in their mission, resulting in the neglect of everything and everyone else around them.

Later Stages of Grief

In the later stages of grief you will begin to find a new normal that seems somewhat comfortable. Obviously you would prefer to go back to the old normal, but since you can't, you begin to view the new normal as an acceptable second best. You still think of your loss fairly often, but the waves of grief are infrequent. You are probably beginning to make your grief work for you by sharing your story, getting involved in support groups and helping others. Holidays are tolerable, and you may even look forward to some of them. The impact of birthdays, death days and anniversaries will lessen, but they will never be forgotten.

As you work through the later stages of grief, you will desire to "start living again." You look forward to things being exciting or thrilling again, but you discover that because of your traumas, the edge is off of life. You have been robbed of your innocence — that ability to trust unconditionally. You will never view life through "rose-colored glasses" again. You are determined to make this experience count, but you feel unsure about yourself. Your confidence may waver.

The Necessity of Grief

Each person will grieve differently and at a different pace, but it is necessary for each person to grieve. Grief will include various combinations of tears, talking, silence, depression, anger, fear, guilt, helplessness and hopelessness, along with a multitude of other emotions. Healthy grief will bring eventual resolution. For some this will come in a few months; for others it will take a few years.

Society seems to feel it is being generous to allow us a year to grieve. Through interviewing many people who are facing the death of a dream, though, I have discovered healing often takes much longer. Recently I read in 2

Samuel 13:38 that it took King David nearly three years to become "consoled concerning Amnon's death" (NIV). If God would allow someone as spiritual as King David to take three years to grieve, surely He will give you and me at least that long.

I have known Jeanette for quite a while. She is a very active, successful woman. One day she shared with me that her mother had died when Jeanette was twelve years old. When she spoke of her mother, tears began to well up in her eyes. Since her mother had been dead for more than twenty years, her tears prompted me to ask some questions. "Were you allowed to grieve for your mother?"

She quickly answered, "Oh, I guess so."

She told me her mother had cancer. Since the family's finances were very limited, they cared for Jeanette's mom at home. Her father and brother were busy in the family business, so much of her mother's care fell on the shoulders of twelve-year-old Jeanette. She was the primary caregiver until shortly before her mother's death when Jeanette's grandparents came and took over the care.

Then I gently asked, "Were you ever able to say goodbye to your mom?"

That question opened a floodgate of unshed tears that Jeanette had been storing up for many, many years.

"No," she answered. "My mother died in the night, and when I woke up in the morning I looked out the window and saw my mother's bedclothes hanging on the line. I ran to her room, and even her hospital bed was gone. All reminders of her were gone, and I didn't even get to say goodbye." Jeanette's mother, her patient, had died when Jeanette wasn't on duty and she felt totally excluded from the death process. There had been no resolution of her feelings.

As Jeanette and I talked further, I suggested she

write down her feelings about her mother's death — not as she perceived the events now as a woman in her early thirties, but the feelings she experienced as a twelve-year-old little girl. The next day we talked through the events she remembered. Then we prayed through those same events, asking God to heal the pain she felt, reveal any other unresolved issues pertaining to her mother's death and give her the strength to deal with them. I then suggested Jeanette spend some time alone in a quiet place, possibly the cemetery, where she could "talk to" her family members, including her mother, about her feelings.

Jeanette had experienced the death of a dream — the dream of having her mother with her through her teenage and adult years to be her advisor and friend and grandmother to her children. She needed a time where she could work through her memories and let go of her dream.

A few days later I was thrilled to receive the following letter from Jeanette:

> I praise God for you, your availability to Him and to me, and your sensitivity in dealing with me. I went home on Wednesday feeling a load had already been lifted from me just by freely sharing after all these years. But I knew I had to keep going. Thursday was hectic and I seemed to be a little fearful of having my talk with my mom and the Lord. Friday I took my kids to their last day of Vacation Bible School and I knew this was my only time alone. For the next hour I talked with God, my mom, my dad and my grandparents. What a total freeing of my mind and heart! I talked with my husband about it and I know I can talk with anyone about all that pain now.

> Another thing that astounds me is that the little "insecure" feeling I have always had deep down is gone! It is hard to believe I experienced that feeling because the grieving part of me was shut up for all those years. This has been a freeing time for me.

If your grief is going on for years and you don't sense any progress, you may be stopped somewhere in the grief process. If you are not sure you have adequately grieved, I would suggest you read my book, *Roses in December.* That book will be helpful in showing you whether you are ready to let go of the past or whether you are still somewhere in the grieving process.

Questions to Ask Yourself

After reading this chapter, which stage of grief would you place yourself in at this point?

Some of the people I have talked with mentioned ways they knew they were beginning to work through their grief:

I laughed out loud and didn't feel guilty.

I spent a length of time in conversation with someone and didn't mention my problem.

I could go to a graduation or wedding without crying.

I could enjoy having sex with my spouse again.

I could be excited for my friends who were pregnant, even though I couldn't have any more children.

My spouse and I could talk about our problem without fighting.

My dread of holidays, birthdays, death days and anniversaries lessened.

I became aware of others' pain and wanted to help.

I realized I came from a dysfunctional family, and I was willing to get help.

Although my parents were far from perfect, I now realize they loved me in the best way they knew how.

List ways you know you are beginning to heal.

2

Letting Go
of Destroyed Dreams

In this chapter we will be discussing *destroyed* dreams, and in the next chapter we will discuss *damaged* dreams. While some situations would fit both categories, I am defining destroyed dreams as those dreams which have ended completely. A permanent physical disability . . . the death of a loved one . . . divorce—the dream is destroyed but the past is not. You've collected memories which include what you've lost. Those memories will be reminders of what used to be, but the old dream cannot be resurrected or reconstructed.

I wish I could invite you in for a cup of coffee, hold your hand, give you a hug, provide you with tissues and have you tell me the story of your destroyed or damaged dream. Recently I invited several of my friends who had experienced alterations and deaths of dreams to my home. We talked about our experiences openly. I'd like to invite you to sit in on our conversation.

Each of us agreed that when our dreams began to fade or die, we grieved. Some of us grieved longer than others, but we all grieved. We also agreed that though we are in different stages of healing, we *are* healing. I asked each of my guests to share some of their healing process, how they knew they were letting go of their dreams and their grief.

Disability

Cornelius is an attractive, well-built black man in his late thirties. His dream was to be an Olympic gymnast, but Vietnam got in the way of his plans. A bullet not only injured his spinal cord and paralyzed his legs, but it also destroyed his dreams.

Cornelius shared his healing process:

For the past three months I helped with a camp for disabled kids operated by the Crippled Children's Society. It's been twenty years since I lost the use of my legs, and I thought I was completely healed. However, during the first session of camp, I went through a grief process. At the end of the camping session, we had a time where all the counselors and campers told one another what they appreciated and learned from the whole week. Some were crying and grieving.

I was crying, too. That's a sign of healing for me because I have not been able to cry in the past. Have you ever had a dream where you were falling and you can't stop yourself? That's the way I felt in that camp session. I knew more grief was working its way out. I knew I had to do something with my pain. I couldn't shut it down. I kept praying and asking God, "Who is going to help me?" God led a young man to me who was able-bodied, with a child-like innocence and acceptance. He was so fresh and so naive and nurturing. I talked to him and shared with him my fears, my anger and my hurt about all of these campers who were institutionalized in a society that doesn't seem to care about disabled people.

"What will happen to all of these children?" I blurted out in frustration. At that moment I recognized and acknowledged my own overwhelming fear that my children might become disabled. I broke down and grieved. I cried out loud like a baby. It was healthy. As I cried, this young man just held me. When I stopped, I had this tremendous peace. If I hadn't gone through that grieving process, I don't believe I would've been able to do the entire five sessions with those disabled kids. My friend let me fall into his arms when I was having the fear of falling into that pain and that pit. I knew I was getting better because this time I had the confidence that God would provide someone to hold me.

I have often wondered, *If I do open up, will anybody hold me? Will they be able to take what I let out?* When I was a child, I dreamed that I was falling, but I always woke up before I hit bottom. In real life we don't know if we're going to hit bottom or not. That fear is so overwhelming that we finally think, *Just let me hit the ground. Let me splatter.* As I let myself fall emotionally, the fear dissipated.

I now have a freedom that I never had before. I don't get headaches and jaw aches from trying to hold down the pain. I finally let that little child inside of me grieve. I didn't realize my fear was so great about my children. I was scared to death that my children would become disabled. I know I'm healing because I can admit my fears.

It is so important to give ourselves permission to feel and release our pain rather than judge ourselves by saying, "What's wrong with you? Why aren't you over this yet?" We need to be willing to admit our fears just as Cornelius did. As we verbalize our fears, we will begin to gain control over them and we can start to let go of our grief.

Cornelius explained that with his injury he often feels he is in the midst of a dream. Although he is paralyzed, he still has feeling in his legs. Because of that feeling, he keeps thinking he may walk again. The reality is that his motor nerves were severed and his feeling nerves weren't. He will never walk again aside from a miraculous healing from God, but sometimes he still plays games with that dream.

Cornelius continued:

> As I listen to others whose dreams have died, the word I hear is *steps*. God took me through the steps of letting go. The first step was facing Vietnamese people. God gave me a job in an unemployment office where I had to help these people find employment or a place to live. I remember coming out of my office one day and meeting this Vietnamese man. He had heard I'd been shot by the South Vietnamese. He hugged me and started crying. I didn't cry with him because I wasn't a crier then, but I was able to receive his hug and his sympathy.
>
> The next step in letting go involved a job where I had to work with other Vietnam vets and constantly listen to their stories. I had to convince them that they had a life ahead of them even though I was still personally dealing with the issue. God gave me the strength and fortitude to do this.

Cornelius took another positive step in the last couple of years when he was finally able to wear shorts and tank tops. Since he lost the use of his legs, he didn't want to look in the mirror. Now he is able to look in the mirror and accept what's there. He is able to go out in public with shorts on. That was a part of accepting his legs as they are now. As he let go of his dream of participating in the Olympics, he was able to build a new dream through performing in some handicapped sports.

His dream to walk again may be destroyed, but his desire to live and serve others grows stronger every day.

Divorce

Sue always dreamed of being a wife, a mother and a missionary. After the birth of twin girls, Sue and her husband became foreign missionaries. It seemed Sue's dreams were coming true — until the day Sue discovered her husband was involved with another woman. Now Sue is back in the States, working as a nurse and raising her girls alone. She frequently drives her girls to a nearby town where they visit their father who is now married to the other woman.

Sue shared she knew she was beginning to heal when she realized that the pit inside of her wasn't bottomless. She could deal with it. It wasn't going to totally overwhelm her or embarrass her in front of anyone else. She knew she was healing when it didn't bother her that other people knew her husband had left their marriage. She began to realize that although the pain was terrible, she wasn't going to die of grief.

Sue recalled:

There were actually two dreams that died when my husband walked out. One of them was the death of a marriage. I had this vision that I was going to be married for the rest of my life. Now that vision was gone. For a long time I had a mental picture of standing at a grave trying to bury my marriage. The hole was dug, but boards were across the grave so they couldn't put the casket down into the ground. The casket was open and they couldn't continue the burial because I refused to throw in my flowers. I was holding a dead wedding bouquet — my symbol of my marriage. I hung on to that bouquet for a long time.

I knew I was beginning to heal when the day came in my vision that I wanted to pick up some fresh pink carnations for myself and throw the dead bouquet into the casket. That's when I knew I was beginning to let go of my grief.

To let go of a marriage, you have to yank it out of your heart, and it took me a long time to be able to do that. My husband consumed me. If I had to call him to talk about the kids, it was a week-long agonizing over, "I'm going to have to call HIM on Friday."

Just yesterday I had to call him. Five minutes before I made the call, I said to my friend, "I'm going to call my ex-husband." My friend was so surprised and said, "You didn't say anything about it this time." I was so peaceful, and it didn't even bother me.

Sue now realizes she had to be able to close the coffin lid on her marriage before she could admit she was single and do something about it. She went on a cruise this summer—a singles cruise. Prior to that she had been terrified of being with single people. But on the cruise she found herself thinking, *This is so much fun. I think I'll do this every time I have a break.* She had a good time and realized she could function in a world which has thousands of single people.

God has renewed her vision for being involved in the divorce recovery group in her church. Sue had gone through all of the training to teach a divorce recovery group, but she couldn't actually do anything with it until she had let go of her dream—her marriage. Now she knows she can survive and enjoy life. She's actually having fun.

Sue also had to let go of her dream to be a missionary. That took a long time. She looked for other jobs, but kept hanging on to her position with the mission organization which she and her husband had served. Once she was able to let go and take another position, she hasn't had to go back. She now sees that God is giving her ministries in many other areas.

Widowhood

Mary Ann was a pastor's wife for thirty-some years. She raised two children and did all the things a pastor's wife is supposed to do. Just as she and her husband were nearing retirement age, he died suddenly. When her husband died, Mary Ann's dreams of spending a long and happy retirement with her husband died. And her identity died, too.

After my husband died, I kept a journal. I counted weeks at first. He died on a Thursday, so every Thursday I wrote how many weeks it had been. Then how many months it had been. Today was Thursday, but today I had to look back to see how long it has been. I'm not counting anymore.

It is typical to be acutely conscious of time, especially in the first few months after a trauma. I recently received a call from a young mother whose baby died of crib death. Her first statement was, "My baby has been dead fifty-eight days." What she was really saying was, "I have existed fifty-eight days without my baby." In one sense, time is our friend because each day we survive separates us a little more from the acute initial pain. But time is also our enemy because each day marks another twenty-four hours since we were able to enjoy our dream.

Mary Ann admitted she doesn't go to the cemetery every week and take flowers anymore. She tried to keep flowers on the grave at first, but now she reasons, "It's so hot; it's a shame to put flowers out there." Before it wouldn't have mattered whether it was hot; she would have had to take flowers.

She said it took a good two years before her husband's death wasn't uppermost in her mind, the first thought every morning. She knew she was beginning to heal when she could sit down and talk to somebody about something else without mentioning she was a widow.

Mary Ann knew she was letting go of her dream of always being a wife when she realized she wanted to be called Mary Ann Alexander rather than Mrs. Henry Alexander.

I wanted to be me. I felt like I was half a person for a good two years. Now I feel I'm a person all by myself.

I couldn't see any good coming out of my situation

like Romans 8:28 mentions, but now I realize I have become a better, stronger person since my husband's death. My husband was a good speaker and very intelligent, and sometimes I felt inferior to him. I miss my husband, but now that he isn't here anymore I am getting to know me.

After her husband's death, Mary Ann went to florist school. The first Christmas she kept herself busy making arrangements. She didn't make much money, but it kept her occupied. The next Christmas she didn't need to keep that busy, but she does make flower arrangements for others frequently. She feels good about herself because she knows she is capable of doing something.

Mary Ann shared:

My husband wanted to climb Mt. San Gorgonio with my son-in-law and our grandsons. The year after Henry's death, my son-in-law and my grandsons did climb the mountain. My daughter and I both wrote letters to my husband and we had the boys put them up on the top of San Gorgonio. My son-in-law sat down and read the letters to his sons and prayed for them and gave them their grandfather's blessing. Writing that letter helped me let go of my dream.

Are You Ready to Let Go?

Do you need to let go of a destroyed dream?

When Francine's husband left her to marry another woman, she didn't want to let go. Even though he was married again, Francine couldn't let go of her dream of a happy marriage and wonderful family.

One weekend my friend Florence was with Francine, and she suggested they conduct a funeral for Francine's dream for her marriage. They knelt in prayer and openly grieved for the dream, for the marriage, and for Francine's pain and feelings of rejection. At that moment,

Francine let the dream die and left it in the Lord's hand to handle as He saw fit. That symbolic funeral was the turning point for Francine. She still struggles with her singleness, her loneliness, and her emotional and material needs, but she has allowed the old dream to remain dead and has given God permission to help her start living in the present rather than dwelling on the past.

Don't feel guilty if after reading this chapter you realize you aren't ready to let go yet. Letting go is a process which usually takes quite a while. After Nathan's death, I grieved for a least a year and a half before I could even start thinking of letting go of my dream and my grief. And I am still in the process of letting go. But I am stronger now than I was last year at this time. I still grieve, but not as often or as long. I am beginning to enjoy holidays more, and I don't dread the anniversary of his death quite so much.

As I was writing this section, the seventh anniversary of Nathan's death occurred. Glen and I didn't plan to go away this year like we usually do. We had just returned from a trip to Australia, and we didn't feel like leaving home again so soon.

Nathan's accident happened on a Thursday evening. This year on that Thursday, although it was two days before the actual date of his death, I began to feel very emotional. Glen and I were lying in bed, and I said, "This may sound silly, but I think I need to go away after all." I turned to Glen and asked, "Are you having a hard time, too, or is it just me?"

There was a long silence. Glen finally said, "It's not just you. Before you mentioned anything, I was lying here thinking, *Seven years ago tonight, at just about this time, we were calling all over trying to find Nate.*"

We held each other tightly and cried together. The next morning I made reservations at a hotel near the beach and we went away. We actually didn't spend much time during the weekend talking about Nate, but we knew we could whenever we felt we needed to. Although I am no longer nurturing or nursing my pain, I do allow myself room to grieve and to avoid situations that would be depressing or discouraging to me.

I didn't expect many of my friends to remember Nate's death date, but I also knew myself well enough to realize if I went to church on Sunday and no one acknowledged my loss, I would be hurt. The best way to spare myself and my friends was to stay away from a potentially hurtful situation. When I came home from that pleasant and relaxing weekend, it was a joy to find that several friends had rememberd with phone calls, cards and flowers.

In the early stages of grief I wanted to hang on to my hurt and my pain. Now I want to let go, and I am letting go more every day. Be patient with yourself. Let yourself grieve as much as you need to. But when the desire comes to let go of the past, be willing to move on.

Questions to Ask Yourself

Describe your dream. What has happened to your dream?

Some of the people I've talked with said they started to let go of their destroyed dreams when:

> *I went to the grave and said a final goodbye.*
>
> *I joined a divorce recovery group.*
>
> *I wrote a letter to my deceased loved one.*
>
> *I cleaned out all of my husband's personal effects and packed them or gave them away.*

List ways you know you are starting to let go of your destroyed dream.

3

Letting Go of Damaged Dreams

Damaged dreams do not die, but they are altered severely. In some ways, damaged dreams are even more difficult to deal with than dreams that have died because there is no permanent end to a damaged dream, no cut-off point where you can close the door on the old dream and start building a new dream. However, damaged dreams are usually salvageable to some extent. There is still hope.

Broken Relationships

Hillary and Chad have two adopted children, a boy and a girl. Hillary was a teacher at a Christian school when their daughter ran away the first time. After she repeatedly ran away and broke the trust that relationships need to be built on, Hillary and Chad had to make the decision that their daughter could not come back home unless major changes were made in her behavior. At the same time Chad's business was floundering, due mainly to his own poor management. Their dreams were crumbling.

Hillary shared how she got through the rough times:

Our issue with our daughter was a matter of trust.

36

That was my loss — a loss of trust in her. We are still experiencing that loss. But as I lost trust in her, I began to grow in my trust in the Lord. The first night she ran away, I came to the realization, "If you can't trust God when it's three o'clock in the morning and your thirteen-year-old daughter is missing, when can you trust Him?" I decided there would never be a better time to start, so I went to bed and went to sleep. The next morning at six, she called us and wanted to come home. That was the beginning of her running and the beginning of my trusting.

Hillary knew she was getting better when she came to the point where she knew others didn't understand and it didn't matter that they didn't understand. She knew she was okay with God and that was all that mattered. She realized then she was well on the way to healing.

Hillary observed that the problems she and Chad had with their daughter turned their marriage around.

Having to deal with her made us deal with our own lives and with our marriage. If we hadn't had to deal with her, I don't know where we would be today.

The last time their daughter left, she had just turned seventeen. Hillary and Chad didn't hear from her for three months. At that point Hillary gave up.

We had done everything we could have done: prayer, searching scriptures, making contracts with her, positive affirmation, stern discipline, gentle discipline, meeting and entertaining her friends, changing schools, home schooling, counselors, consistent attendance at church and youth group, etc.

When I gave up, Psalm 131 became my solace. I pictured myself as a weaned child, one who demands nothing, climbing on God's lap and sitting there quietly, confident in His love for me and His ability to handle this situation.

Hillary pictured this in her mind over and over for the next couple of months. Later she realized this was a period of grief. She released all her dreams for her daughter and let them go. Today, when Hillary's thoughts go back to what might have been, she has to consciously remember that her confidence is in God and that He is to be trusted with all our lives.

Hillary concluded:

> Both our children have been a blessing to us. Our son, in his wisdom and obedience, has blessed us and in turn he experiences the blessing in receiving the approval of God and men. Our daughter has blessed us in causing Chad and me to seek God and His healing for our lives and our marriage. Someday we trust she will put herself in the position to experience the blessing of God's love too.
>
> Once I let go of my dream for our daughter, God gave me His strength to go on. He has met my needs.

Chad shared his thoughts:

> I thought I was through all of this pain and everything was cool. But when Marilyn mentioned what we were going to do here tonight, I started getting mental pictures of my daughter in a white wedding dress and I was walking her down the aisle. I didn't even know I had dreams like that anymore. I guess I'm still healing.
>
> One of the real hurdles for me was when our daughter had been gone for a long time. She came back and promised she was going to abide by the rules of the house. Three days later she met some guy at the park and took off for the weekend. When she came home, I had to say, "I'm sorry. We can't have you here."
>
> I packed her stuff and took her back where she had been staying. That's when my letting go started.

Sharing the Burden of Shattered Dreams

Joan and Don raised five children, became financially successful, served in a full-time Christian ministry, and were both active in the leadership of their church. When their youngest daughter rebelled against the standards of their home, becoming sexually active outside of marriage and eventually pregnant, Joan and Don experienced the death and damage of several dreams. The relationship with their precious daughter was broken; their hopes for her future were, at the least, sidetracked; and their dear little grandchild was adopted into another family.

In the past few years, Don has also experienced financial reversals which have plunged him into unexpected debt and created some dramatic vocational changes for him.

Joan shared her feelings:

> I know one of the things that contributed to my healing was the decision to not keep what was happening to us a private matter. That was a hard decision because I grew up always wanting to help and please people. I wanted to make a difference in my world. To admit seeming failure, that I have a child who is going berserk according to my goals and values, was a difficult thing to let be known. I know I shared our story with some people who would rather have not known, but that's the chance you take. And once I shared openly that our daughter had left home, was living with a man, and was pregnant, I had a lot of people praying.
>
> The comfort that I was willing to accept from God was part of my healing too. I could choose *not* to be comforted. I could find comfort in any number of things, but I have to *choose* to be comforted.

Don remembered:

> Hillary and Chad were the first couple to call us and

say, "Come on over for dinner." When their daughter had run away years before, I had thought, *Why is she teaching in a Christian school when she has a kid who behaves this way?* I thought somewhat less of Chad too. I assumed they blew it someplace along the line. Now I say, "Hey, we're one of them!" Hillary and Chad were just wonderful and they helped us begin to heal.

Joan and I were tough. We had been raised in the midwest mindset: "Never admit you hurt." Well, we did hurt, and we hurt deeply. I had a friend who was going through the same thing at the same time, and he and I got together every noon for months and prayed. Finally we began to heal as we realized we had done everything we knew how. I'm sure we made mistakes raising all of our kids, but we did what we thought was right.

For the first few weeks, my wife and I didn't want to go to church. Now I can go to church and I don't worry what others think. I know I'm healing because I don't even think about what they're thinking of me.

When our daughter was still home and doing the wrong things, our counselor told Joan and me that we had to agree. We had to be one in how we dealt with her. I would say, "Well, we ought to do this to her as punishment," and Joan would say, "No, we can't do that." As the dad, it seemed I was always the tough guy and Joan always fixed things up. It really helped us to heal when we stopped fighting each other and began to agree on our actions.

We were finally able to release our daughter to the Lord because we saw more happen when we prayed than from listening to all the advice in the world. The support from friends was great. We needed their support.

But now it seems like we don't have the support that we did when we were in the midst of our problem. Actually, we're *still* in the midst of it. The baby is born and has been adopted, but our daughter isn't reconciled to God or to our family. I know, though, that God does hear and answer our prayers. One day we're going to see our daughter come back. I don't think I've experienced the death of a dream; it's just been delayed and altered. We're still in the process, but we have peace.

Joan shared her letting go experience:

I have had to let go of the visual pictures of our daughter and what she might have been. Someday she may still be some of that, but she will never be the young innocent girl she was in my dreams.

I had to allow God to change my perspective on what the future could be for our daughter. I always say, "Lord, anything You want," and then I present Him with this rigid little plan that I want Him to implement. I have received encouragement in letting Him redirect our lives when I think of a person like Chuck Colson. He could never be what he is today except for what he went through. When I think of how God is using people like Chuck Colson today, I get excited about what the future might be for our daughter.

Don commented:

I am seeing how faithful God is. Every knothole I go through, I see He is faithful. I almost look forward to what is going to happen next so I can see God's faithfulness. He stretches our character and our vision. We are learning to say, "Thank you, Lord," in advance because sometimes in the middle of it, you can't.

This past summer Joan and Don decided to get on with what God has called them to do rather than camp in their muddle. They kept involved in their church care group, went calling on church visitors and made an effort to reach out to new people in the congregation. They also had many opportunities to share the gospel with people. They are working at getting on with life in spite of their personal circumstances.

As I listened to these dear parents who have had to let go of the original dream for their children while still tightly grasping the hope for reconstruction of a damaged dream, I was reminded of the scripture where Jesus looked longingly over Jerusalem and said, "O Jerusalem, Jerusalem . . . how often would I have gathered thy children together, as a hen doth gather her brood under her wings, and ye would not" (Luke 13:34, KJV). He, too, experienced the death of a dream, but He is still calling out to Jerusalem, His children. He, too, is holding a damaged dream.

Dreams for a Family

Although it's not possible for all of us to chat in person, some of you have taken the time to write to me and have given me permission to share your dreams in this book. You've also given me hope as you've shared how you picked up the pieces and began again.

Margie writes:

> My dream was to have a really close family as my children grew up and a very special relationship with my grandchildren when they came along.
>
> In his late teens, my son (the oldest of two children) went out of state, became a hippie, finally settled down and married a girl from that area. He lives one thousand miles away and I see my two grandchildren once or twice a year. We don't have a lot of contact, but they know I love them.
>
> My daughter was at home until age twenty-three and we were very close. She married a local boy (a child of an alcoholic) who has tried to isolate her from her family. God has given them two lovely children, one born on my birthday. I thought, *Here it comes; that special relationship I've longed for!* But even though they are only ten miles away, I only get to see them about once a month. I had the idea that my grandchildren would always be in and out of my home and life all the time. I am disappointed by the way things have turned out. I wanted

so badly to be a good grandmother and help to have some influence in my grandchildren's spiritual training. God has not allowed me to do this.

I needed something to fill the void, so the Lord gave me the privilege of helping to start a new church. During that first year, we had eleven new babies born in our congregation. I spent almost every Sunday that first eighteen months in the nursery and many of those babies now call me Grandma Margie. I have a love relationship with them that helps them and me.

The Lord said, "As you have done it to the least of these, you have done unto me." These children are not the "least" by any means, but God has given me the opportunity to model for them a loving and caring adult. Many of them have no grandparents in the area and I enjoy substituting for a little while.

Margie's original dream has not come true, but she has allowed God to heal her enough so she is able to make room for new and altered dreams in her life.

Childhood Abuse

Some of you may be in the process of recognizing you have been working with a wrong set of directions or faulty information concerning yourself, your family and your childhood.

Heather thought she came from a wonderful family where everyone seemed to be in step except her. She knew she was a victim of abuse, but little Heather reasoned that those things must be happening to her because she was bad. She didn't deserve to have good things happen. As Heather grew older, she started spending her time with the "undesirables" at school, reasoning that good kids wouldn't want to spend time with her — she was bad. As a teenager she was promiscuous and got pregnant. She had an abortion because she wouldn't be a good mother — she was a bad person. Heather experienced several failed marriages before she went for counseling in desperation, saying, "Why am I so bad?"

Through intensive counseling Heather began to realize she had been given faulty information about herself. Her counselor has helped her realize she is precious to God; she did not start out as a bad or inferior person. Bad things happened to her, but she was not bad. Heather has had to grieve over her lost childhood and start writing new information about herself.

While it is healthy for us to grieve over our destroyed or damaged dreams, it can become unhealthy if we aren't eventually able to bring our grief to a conclusion and let go of our dream or accept an altered version.

The poem which is used to open this section (see p. 10) was sent to me by my friend Tricia. She writes:

> This was on a bookmark I found five years ago when I was struggling through the abuse I endured as a child. I had always dreamed of a perfect childhood and in realizing that it would never be, I finally let go of my dream.
>
> It was then that I began to heal. I was ready to allow God to do His healing in my life. And it was then that I began to experience the "perfect" childhood I had always wanted, only this time God was the Father.

Financial Devastation

I mentioned earlier that Don and Joan have also experienced many financial changes. Don reflected on the lessons learned:

> A turning point for me was when I was forced to learn biblical principles in the area of finances. I understood the Spirit-filled life concept for a good number of years, and everything came up roses financially for me. It seemed I couldn't make a mistake.

God had to teach me that not only does He give, but He's in control and He can give it back or He can take it away. It's been a gradual thing and I've been able to learn tremendous things that I wish I had known when I was nineteen years old.

In the past I had everything a person could ever dream of having and it was all basically paid for as far as farmland in the midwest and then a move to California. I did some land exchanges and got involved in high-tech California agriculture. We were in the middle of some development projects when President Reagan decided that the farmer had to pay his own way. We saw land prices drop in half and the interest rate on our million dollar loan rise from 10 to 22 percent. We just got over the hump when a hailstorm destroyed everything overnight. The next year we had double crops, but so did everybody else in the world, so prices were half and it cost us twice as much to pick it, ship it, pack it and everything else.

Now I'm confined to 480 square feet and I am binding books. There was a time I used to walk on a thousand acres and feel confined, but now I'm having so much fun working with my hands. I have to spend forty hours a week in a little bitty place and do so many books or I'm not going to make it. We're selling our house to try to pay down farm debt and get the thing turned around. The thing God teaches me is that He is in control. If the Lord can take care of the sparrow, He can take care of us.

Once I let go and turned my situation over to God, He then gave me the opportunity to teach financial seminars through our church. Now I really enjoy teaching biblical principles to young kids who are just starting out.

Chad commented:

I don't know how many years I sat in my shop knowing what the experts said about the way you are supposed to run a business and thinking, *I don't have to do it that way. It's going to be different for me. Something is going to happen and everything's going to come together.* The turnaround has come since I've stopped daydreaming and really started working in the business.

As Chad learned, we must be willing to release the energy we are using in trying to hang on to the old dream and channel that energy into building new dreams.

Sudden Unemployment

As long as I have known Wayne, he has been a successful businessman. About two years ago he left an executive position in a Christian company and moved his family to another city where he assumed a prominent position in another Christian company. After nine months in that job, his world crashed around him. Wayne recalled:

> It was the worst day of my life. I had never been "fired," "laid off" or "canned" from a job. I had never been ahead of sales plan, ahead of schedule, ahead of everything, and been let go. I was humiliated, scared and downright mad!
>
> But the worst was yet to come. Life was not going to be the same from that point on. I had to go home and tell my wife and family that I no longer had a job. They look up to me, depend on me and support me. Now, in my mind, I had failed them.
>
> I got home, and my wife immediately sensed what I was going to say. She was extremely caring and supportive from the start.
>
> Next, we had to tell the children. We shared our feelings with them and allowed them to air their feelings and come to terms with what might happen in the future. Together we prayed as a family. My son had the best prayer: "Whenever God closes a door, He opens a window." I was too hurt and angry to see his wisdom, but later, as the pieces came together, he was right. God opened a wonderful window for us.

My personal hurt and anger continued to burn. It was very hard to forgive these people. Two separate events helped.

First, I met with the man who hired me and confronted him with the facts and, most importantly, my feelings. It was an intense meeting but it helped me emotionally. As we talked, I could feel some empathy from him and a great deal of concern. I had prayed hard that my words would be anointed by God, and they were. This person ultimately helped my job search by giving me a fine letter of introduction. He later gave my new employer an above-average reference. I don't believe I could have forgiven him, nor would he have assisted me in my job search, without this meeting.

Second, I met with the company president. This was very difficult, but again I shared the facts and the emotions. He is not an emotional man, but I let him know what his decision had done to my family as well as my "dream." This meeting cleared the air and I could sense some remorse on his part. He also worked with me to help me find a new position. I was able to forgive him and move on with what I had to do.

Realizing we had to grieve was an important step to living again. We shed tears at strange times, we got a little depressed, and something was missing in our lives (intangible things like security, life-patterns, etc.). We missed the "good ol' days" which at times added to our sense of loss and caused us to second guess our decision to make the move in the first place, "Why did I change jobs?" "If only we would have . . . "

The only way to climb out of this grief was to use our strengths. I began to see some fruit from my job search — my hard work was beginning to pay off. My wife analyzed the details and logically put the pieces back together. The times we were using our strengths were the best for us.

Uncertain Health

I shared some of Helen's story in the first chapter. Helen faced the death of a dream when her musical career was ended by multiple sclerosis. She also faced many damaged dreams because of the physical limitations caused by the MS.

Helen writes of the alteration of her life plans:

> I felt my life was over. I was put on massive doses of cortisone, and I gained seventy pounds. But eventually I began to feel better! I couldn't put in a full day's work, but if I planned my rest periods, I had many productive hours. Although I knew my future was uncertain, I prayed for something to do.
>
> I signed up for a braille transcribing course for the sighted, and I really threw myself into it. In six months I earned my Literary Transcriber's Certificate from the Library of Congress and began a course in music braille.
>
> I had a few opportunities to braille for some of the blind members of our community, but it wasn't until I followed up on a conversation with a friend about Lutheran Braille Workers that I began to see where this new knowledge was leading. LBW is the largest producer of Christian braille in the world, serving 110 countries in more than forty languages, and they needed volunteer transcribers.
>
> That "chance" conversation has led to more than twelve years of the most challenging, interesting and rewarding work possible. I have done much of the work in my home at my own pace. I began as a "hand transcriber," one who does special-request braille items such as Sunday school lessons for a group of blind children in Jamaica or a devotional book for a library in India.
>
> LBW installed an electro-mechanical machine in our church that embosses braille on metal plates for mass production. That machine is now in a special room in our

home. Each plate may be used to produce at least 10,000 copies. I will soon have embossed 10,000 plates (20,000 pages) from both manuscripts that I have transcribed myself and those supplied to me from the various Bible societies or missionary groups in other countries.

What wonderful responses come from these groups and the schools, churches, and blind individuals who receive our books, especially those who have never before had personal access to the Scriptures! I now have "pen pals" in Tanzania, Australia, Ghana, Switzerland, India, Germany, England, Hong Kong and the Philippines, among others.

Those who have shared in this chapter are dealing with altered or damaged dreams rather than dreams which have been completely destroyed. They can look at their situations as hopeless, or they can pick up the broken pieces and accept a new version of the old dream. In the "Living Again" section, you will hear how some of these people have used the remaining portions of their old dreams to help them build new dreams and learn to live again.

If you sense it is time to let go of your dream, but something is holding you back, please pay close attention to the next chapter. Maybe God doesn't want you to say goodbye to your dream just yet. With myself, I had to walk through the process of forgiveness several times before I was ready to let go. As you read the next few pages, I pray your heart will be ready to listen if God has a special message for you.

Questions to Ask Yourself

Would you define your dream as damaged or destroyed?

Do you feel you are ready to start letting go or do you feel stuck in the process?

Some of the people I've talked with said they started to let go of their damaged dreams when:

> *I wrote a letter (but never sent it) to the person who molested me, saying exactly how I felt as a child and as an adult.*

> *Through a process of counseling, I was able to release myself from feeling responsible for others' decisions.*

> *I started to allow my family the room to make mistakes and be human.*

List ways you know you are starting to let go of your damaged dream.

4

Letting Go
of Unforgiveness

I know many of you have been deeply hurt and forgiveness is a tough topic to talk about. Through the pain of watching the death or alteration of a dream, though, I'm sure we all have somebody we need to forgive of something.

The morning after Nathan died, someone came into my home and said, "Have you forgiven him yet?"

"Who?" I asked.

"The drunk driver," the person replied.

I responded, "I don't know. I don't have time to deal with him. I have to bury my son."

This person was very determined that I should go to the hospital, see the drunk driver and tell him I forgive him. I refused to go at that time, and the person regarded my refusal as unforgiveness. That really wasn't true. I just wasn't dealing with him yet. People often unfairly judge our spirituality by how quickly we are able to forgive.

What Is Forgiving?

First of all, let's define *forgiving*. The dictionary says it is "the act of giving up resentment of a person or giving up the claim to requital." *Requital* means to make payment. I've come to define *forgiving* as giving up our claim to avenge a wrongdoing. The key in forgiving is the act of *voluntarily* giving up resentment or revenge.

It is just as important to know what forgiving is *not*. Forgiving is *not* necessarily forgetting. You hear people say, "I can forgive, but I can't forget." Somehow we have the idea that if you haven't forgotten, you haven't really forgiven. It is not likely that we will ever be able to forget what has happened, but it is possible to remember and still forgive. I imagine most of us will always remember the feelings we had the moment our dream began to die.

Dr. Lewis B. Smedes says, "We should not make forgetting a test of our forgiving. The test of forgiving lies with healing the lingering pain of the past, not with forgetting that the past ever happened."[1]

Remembering the event and even the anger you felt does not necessarily mean you have not forgiven. I still get angry every time I read about a drunk driver. I pace around my house and stomp and storm because drunk driving is a crime and it should not be allowed. But I am not filled with the kind of anger that would cause me to go out and do harm to the man who killed my son or to other drunk drivers. I still would like to lock them up, but I don't want to hurt them physically. Those feelings do not consume my life to the point where I can't go on and do other things.

Forgiveness and Justice

Just recently Oprah Winfrey broadcast a program on forgiving. Her guest, Janice Harris Lord, said we need to understand that "forgiveness is not a replacement for justice."[2] That is a very important concept. Some of you may be victims of deliberate, illegal acts such as wrongful death, murder, drunk driving, abuse or willful malpractice situations. Just because you have forgiven the perpetrator doesn't mean you wouldn't want to see him or her go to jail. You do not have to feel guilty if you hope the person will have to pay the judicial price, that which the law decrees, for what he did.

Those who are victims of divorce are often made to feel guilty if they use legal means to obtain child support or alimony. Once the divorce courts have decreed a settlement and custody arrangement, both parties have a legal and moral obligation to meet the terms of that agreement. If one party breaks the agreement, the other party has the right to ask for help from the court system. To do so does not indicate unforgiveness.

Forgiveness Is a Process

My friend Sue commented:

When it comes to forgiveness and divorce, I don't believe it's a once-for-all thing. Also, it's really difficult to forgive until you can admit there was a wrong committed or a problem that needs forgiveness.

For ten years I denied there were any problems or wrongdoings in our marriage. All the abuse and lack of care, nurturing and affection were denied year after year. When our marriage did break up and the abuse was acknowledged, I still was unable to place responsibility appropriately. I continued to assume it was my responsibility in some way.

Actually, forgiveness is a process for me. The pain, hurt and wrongdoing have to be dealt with one piece at a time. For me, there are parts of my broken marriage relationship that I have been able to work through to complete that process. Others I'm still working on. Unfortunately, in a divorce situation, there are new ones cropping up all the time because as long as there are children, issues will continue to come up and need to be processed and forgiven.

Here it is, almost four years since our divorce was

final, and this last week I was having to forgive my former husband *again* for leaving us, for putting me in a position where I have to work full time and take responsibility for being both chief and only bread winner and nurturer for my children. I have to be both mother and father to them and bear responsibilities far beyond God's plans or intentions.

On the other hand, I have been able to work through and forgive my former husband for his unfaithfulness in our marriage. After some help I was able to finally accept those things, place responsibility where it belonged and let those things go. No, I haven't forgotten, but I am not reliving the pain each time I see him.

Forgiveness has no timetable. Sometimes we think, "Isn't it wonderful that they were able to go right away and tell this man that they forgave him?" If people can't do that, we assume they aren't quite as spiritual as they should be. I think people who believe this idea may be the ones who are kidding themselves.

If I had gone to the drunk driver the first day and said, "I forgive you," I might have been sincere, but I wouldn't have understood what I was saying. I didn't even know what I had to forgive him of yet. Two years, five years, seven years later, I know what I have to forgive; I understand what he has deprived me of. The first day I didn't realize all the things I would never experience because somebody decided to drink and drive. The graduations, the wedding, the grandchildren—those hadn't hit me yet.

If forgiveness is premature, it may not be real.

Why Do We Need to Forgive?

Is forgiveness necessary? For the Christian, the Bible teaches it is. God gives us the ultimate example: He gave His only Son to provide forgiveness and salvation for us. The Bible says that even Christ forgave the people who crucified Him when He was blameless. And Christ teaches that we are to forgive others as He forgave us. If we go to the altar and we remember we have feelings against a brother, we are told to go take care of that problem before we try to come to the Lord. We are to forgive, but I also think He allows time to work on it.

When we refuse to forgive, we remain in bondage to the person who hurt us. Unforgiveness also deprives us of the opportunity to use our hurt and experience in a positive way. I have watched many people permit unforgiveness and resentment to eat away at their souls and render them totally helpless and unproductive in their spiritual and personal lives. The person who *really* loses when unforgiveness occurs is the one who is unwilling to forgive.

How Do We Forgive?

How do we go about forgiving? First of all, we have to be willing to forgive. Sometimes we have to say, "Lord, I'm willing to be made willing. I know that's what You're asking, but Lord, don't You know what that person did? Did You hear what he said to me? Did You sense his attitude?"

The Lord says, "Just be willing or be willing to be made willing, and I'll work with you."

Admit Our Pain

When we are willing to walk the path toward forgiveness, we must start with admitting our pain and our hurt. As Christians, so often we have a tendency to think we're more spiritual if we don't admit how much we hurt and if we don't acknowledge the anger that's inside us. That's not true. Hiding our anger is not spiritual. It is lying if you don't admit the pain that's inside of you. Give it to God and say, "Lord, see the pain in me. I feel so hurt."

Dr. Smedes says, "The hurt that creates a crisis of forgiving has three dimensions. It is always personal, unfair, and deep. When you feel this kind of three-dimensional pain, you have a wound that can be healed only by forgiving the one who wounded you."[3]

There are hurts that cause us to say, "Yes, someone killed my dream. This is a personal thing." Unfair? Oh yes. Many times the happenings in our lives are unfair. For myself, to have two babies die and a third child killed — that's certainly unfair.

Deep? My pain went all the way through me. It's that kick-in-the-stomach kind of pain which makes you double over because it hurts so bad. At that point you know you're at the "crisis of forgiving." You have to decide, Am I going to forgive or not? You need to try to verbalize how you feel either by writing or talking about it. Talk your feelings into a tape recorder or find a good friend who will let you yell and holler when you need to.

Let Out the Feelings

After talking about feelings and admitting them, we have to allow them to come out. Dr. Smedes talks about this stage of the process: "You cannot shake the memory of how much you were hurt, and you cannot wish your enemy well. You sometimes want the person who hurt you to suffer as you are suffering."[4]

You can express your feelings through journalizing, or isolating yourself in a room and shouting, screaming, crying or even punching a pillow. I have a teddy bear I can carry around. I'm nice to him, but when I have hard days I really hug my teddy. That may sound strange, but it has worked wonders. I don't carry him around very often anymore, but for a while I carried him a lot. My little teddy bear and I have had some good conversations. He was something to hug, something I could cry with and he didn't reproach me. My bear can't talk back, and that's good. You may need outlets like that.

It is important that you focus your anger on the right object. When we try to suppress our anger, it often comes pouring out on innocent victims. Jan Frank, an incest victim and the author of *A Door of Hope,* relates:

> In my own life, I began to exhibit outbursts of anger months before I was aware I had a problem in this area. I was angry with my boss when he overruled a decision I made. I was angry at a speeding driver. I was angry at a young boy who trespassed on our property. I was angry at my husband for pouring too much cereal for my daughter's breakfast. I was angry at my toddler for crying for "no good reason." In psychological terms, the anger was being displaced — directed at someone or something other than the true source.[5]

It seldom works just to say, "I shouldn't be this angry," and have it go away instantly. There needs to be a release valve where you can let anger out in a constructive, controlled manner.

Candy Lightner, the founder of Mothers Against Drunk Driving, did an excellent job of focusing her anger. She was angry at those who chose to drink and drive and at the justice system which did not prosecute drunk drivers sufficiently. Because she channeled her anger in a positive and productive way, she was able to organize one of the most effective public awareness campaigns in history.

Identify the Offenders

To focus on the area of forgiveness, you need to acknowledge or identify the offender or offenders. I made a list of the people with whom I was really angry. There actually were more than I thought. Besides the drunk driver and friends who had offended me, I finally acknowledged I was angry at God.

There came a point when I needed to forgive God. God in Himself never needs forgiveness, but there are times in our lives when from our point of view things look so unfair, so hurtful, that we need to say, "God, I forgive You. I don't understand. From my vantage point, it seems You really hurt me. I know You have a purpose, and You have the road map, but I don't. I can't always see Your plan, and from my point of view, it doesn't make a whole lot of sense." It is not sacrilegious to say, "God, I forgive You." It is an exercise we may need to go through to get back on speaking terms with God and acknowledge the severe pain we have gone through.

After Nathan's death, I also had to forgive myself. Some of you may have to go through that too, especially if you were involved in the incident which caused your pain. "Why didn't I see it coming? Why didn't I know? Why didn't I sense it?"

I wasn't with Nathan the night he was killed, so I kept thinking, *Why didn't I go to that basketball game with him?* Though I wouldn't have been riding with him if I had gone, it was different than normal that I didn't go. So I reasoned that must be why it happened. I failed. I wasn't a good parent that night. I didn't go to the basketball game.

I was a great parent, and I knew it at the time. But for a while, I kept thinking, *Why didn't I pay more attention? If I had known . . .* I finally had to say, "Marilyn, if there's anything you've done wrong, I forgive you." I just had to look myself in the mirror and say, "I know you're a nice lady. I know you love Nathan. You did everything you could. If you made mistakes, I forgive you."

There was yet another person I had to forgive. I went through a day of prayer and emotional healing with a group called Philippian Ministries.

I spent a morning talking through my life. Then in

the afternoon the prayer director worked with me and we prayed through different situations. I talked with God about significant people in my life and asked forgiveness for wrong things I had done toward them. During this time the director asked if I could tell God that I forgave Nathan for dying.

I just about jumped out of my chair. I said, "It wasn't his fault!"

She said, "I know that, but can you forgive him for dying?"

"Well, of course, because it wasn't his fault!"

She said, "Fine. Why don't you say that to God?"

I tried to say it, but I couldn't get it out. It took me a long time. I sat there and cried and prayed. Finally, the first words that came out were, "Nate, why'd you leave me so soon?" I realized I was mad at him. I know that's not logical, but I can guarantee some of you are also mad at an innocent party. You may be thinking, *Couldn't you have noticed the danger? Couldn't you sense you were in trouble? Couldn't you have done something different? Couldn't you have prevented the divorce? Why didn't you try harder to please the boss so you wouldn't lose your job? You shouldn't have risked our money on those bad investments. Why didn't you take better care of yourself? You should have noticed that lump sooner.*

Many times as I went down the freeway I would look at the exit Nate took the night of the accident, and I would think, *Nate, why didn't you take Waterman instead of Del Rosa? Couldn't you have done better? Couldn't you see that car coming? Why didn't you get there a little sooner or a little later?* All of those things may seem silly now, yet I needed to release my feelings and admit there was something that made me mad at Nate even though I loved him and would have given my life for him.

As you go through this process with each person you need to forgive, you may need to confront some individuals personally. If you feel you do, that's all right, but get a lot of wise counsel before you do so. I have not had the opportunity to confront the drunk driver and have never felt God was leading me in that direction. However, I have put a chair in the middle of the room and imagined that the man who killed my son was sitting there. I have imagined that others who have said hurtful things each sat in that chair. I have talked to each of them in the privacy of my room and of my mind. I have told them how I felt.

Accepting the Results

Once we have followed this procedure and asked for or given forgiveness, we must accept the results. After you say, "Lord, I forgive" you must remember forgiveness does not necessarily guarantee the other person will change.

I have a humorous story to illustrate how I learned things don't always change just because your attitude does.

My son Matthew is a wonderful young man. When he was in high school, he was a model Christian teenager. He did everything just the way a young boy should. He was a valedictorian of his senior class, earned a 4.0 GPA, and won a scholarship to a major university in California. We were so proud of him. Then he went away to college and things changed a little bit. He became rather individualistic. He didn't do everything quite the way his parents had done before him.

One day he was marching in the college band down a street in San Francisco. One of his white tennis shoes came untied and fell off. What was he supposed to do? He couldn't say, "Stop the band. I need to go back and get my tennis shoe." So he kept marching.

When he got home, he bought a new pair of blue

tennis shoes. As he started to put the blue shoes on, he looked over at the remaining white shoe and thought, *It's too bad to throw that shoe away. It's not worn out yet.* So he decided to wear one white shoe and one blue shoe. That was fine with me as long as he stayed at school. But then he came home, and he still wanted to wear one white shoe and one blue shoe.

Well, you can imagine what this did to the "Heavilin image." We attended a rather straight-laced church, and whenever Matt walked into the service behind me, I would see people give a quick glance at his shoes and smirk. I felt they were thinking, *She's getting hers now!* I wanted to run away. I was embarrassed. I found when Matt would say, "I've got homework. I don't think I'll go to church with you tonight," I would say, "That's okay, honey. You can stay home if you want to."

Normally that would never be acceptable at our house. When we went to church, everyone went to church. But now it was acceptable; I was almost relieved when he didn't come.

Then one day the Lord said to me, *Marilyn, what's more important—that Matt wear matched shoes or that he go to church with you and learn about Me?* Well, when the Lord put it to me like that, I had to admit those shoes didn't matter quite as much as I thought they did. God said, *You've been giving Matt the wrong impression. You're teaching him that things are important which shouldn't be important. You haven't been showing him that his life and soul are what matters. You've taught him that shoes and measuring up to what people expect are more important than I am. You need to go ask his forgiveness and talk to him about this.*

I said, "Matt, I have to apologize. It has really bugged me that you've worn mismatched shoes. I want to ask your forgiveness."

He said, "Oh, that's okay."

Then I thought, *Now that I've asked for forgiveness, he'll wear matched shoes.* But he didn't! And for three years after that he wore two different-color tennis shoes. That's what can happen sometimes. Even after we've tried to improve a situation, nothing seems to change.

This is a trivial story, but it does have a great ending. Matt is now thirty. He is an executive in a computer company. He wears a three-piece suit, a white shirt, a tie and matched shoes. He and his mom have an excellent relationship.

While this story is simple, we need to realize that the principle is important. The man who killed my son, whom I have forgiven, has been arrested for drunken driving several times since Nathan's death. Each time I hear stories about him, I have to go back and work this out a little more: *Did you really mean it, Marilyn? Will you mean it if you read in the headlines that he's killed someone else?* I'll have to work on that if it ever happens. We must recognize that the people we forgive do not change automatically because of our forgiveness.

Forgiveness Can Change You

While forgiveness may not change the person you're forgiving, it will definitely have an effect in your life.

Stormie Omartian, a woman who was badly abused as a child by her mother, stated, "Forgiveness doesn't make the other person right; it just makes you free."[6] The person who is truly liberated is you.

I discovered a special verse in the book of Job recently. Job is certainly one who went through many trials. We look at him and there aren't many of us who can compare with his sufferings even though we have had some difficult times. Job also had what we now refer to as "Job's comforters," the men who came to counsel Job on his difficulties. They said the dumbest things, and they didn't help him at all. They sat there and told him everything he had done wrong. They were sure Job had all kinds of sin in his life.

We have "Job's comforters" come to us too, don't we? Oswald Chambers states, "To be able to explain suffering is the clearest indication of never having suffered."[7] People don't mean to hurt us, but they sure say dumb and hurtful things sometimes.

Yet in chapter 42 of Job it says, "Then, when Job prayed for his friends, the Lord restored his wealth and happiness!" (Job 42:10, TLB)

"After Job prayed for his friends!" It took me a long time, but I have gotten to the point where I can pray for the man who killed my son. Sometimes the Lord must chuckle at my prayers: "Lord, if he's drunk, get him arrested." But I also pray, "Lord, bring someone into his life who will help him straighten up. Let him see that You're the answer."

I am praying the Lord will win that man to Himself. I believe someday I may see him in heaven and I can be happy about it. Please note, I still want him to pay for whatever he does wrong. Our feelings of forgiveness and our desire for justice are not a contradiction.

Dr. Smedes states, "When you release the wrongdoer from the wrong, you cut a malignant tumor out of your inner life. You set a prisoner free, but you discover that the real prisoner was yourself."[8]

That is really true. We may not be able to control the other person or the event, but we can control what's happening within ourselves. As we willingly let God peel away a layer of unforgiveness, we may be surprised at what is revealed.

When the day comes that we meet our precious Lord Jesus, I trust we can say, "We did the best we knew how with what You gave us." Forgiveness is a tough one, but when you walk through it, you see that His light can shine through as we claim the ability to forgive. It may not make a difference in the lives of those we choose to forgive, but it will make all the difference in the world in ours because we are released from the bondage of unforgiveness.

Although I may not discuss your particular type of broken dream in this book, I hope you are able to identify with others' stories as they describe the hurt, the disillusionment, the breaking of trust, and the devastation that comes with the destruction or damage of a dream. I pray that you will walk with each of us as we work through the fear of letting go of a dream, find the desire to launch out and dream again, and accept the reality of living with new dreams.

Questions to Ask Yourself

If this chapter made you feel a little uncomfortable, why don't you take time right now to talk with God? As you are talking with Him, ask Him to help you answer the following questions.

Am I mad at God? If so, take time right now to at least initiate a conversation with Him regarding this issue. Tell Him why you're upset. Ask Him to help you resolve your feelings of anger, bitterness or unforgiveness.

Am I mad at myself? Write down all the reasons you are upset with yourself. Then, when you are ready, talk to God in prayer and ask Him to help you forgive yourself. After you have done that, write FORGIVEN across your list.

Am I mad at others? Ask God to bring to mind anyone who has hurt you in the past whom you haven't forgiven. Write their names down. Pray over each name and ask God to give you the strength to forgive each person by name.

Do I need to ask forgiveness of others? Ask God to bring to mind anyone you have hurt in the past from whom you should ask forgiveness. Write their names down. Pray over each name and ask God to give you the strength to deal with each person in a way directed by God.

Launching Out

Launch Out

The mercy of God is an ocean divine,
A boundless and fathomless flood:
Launch out in the deep, cut away the shoreline,
And be lost in the fullness of God.

O many, alas, only stand on the shore,
And gaze on the ocean so wide;
They never have ventured its depths to explore
Or to launch on the fathomless tide.

And others just venture away from the land,
And linger so near to the shore,
The surf and the slime that beat over the strand
Sweep o'er them their floods evermore.

O let us launch out on this ocean so broad
Where floods of salvation o'erflow;
O let us be lost in the mercy of God
Till the depths of His fullness we know.

                     —A. B. Simpson[1]

5

Launching Out
to God

Often when people are facing severe trauma, we'll hear statements such as,

"I don't understand God."

"How could a loving God allow such a nice person to suffer so terribly?"

"I never thought God would allow this to happen."

I hadn't argued with God when Jimmy died. I reasoned that everyone has some troubles in their lives. Why should I expect to go untouched? When I learned I was expecting twins, it was easy to rationalize that I had "passed the test" and God was repaying me for the child who had died.

However, when Ethan died, God wasn't operating according to my program any longer. He wouldn't fit into my box. I had lots of questions.

In the seventeen years between Ethan's and Nathan's deaths, I went through a process of re-evaluating God. I discovered the God I knew up to that point wasn't really the God portrayed in Scripture.

Defining God According to Scripture

The God of Scripture allows bad things to happen to good people. Acts 7 tells us of the death of Stephen: "Then [the crowd] cried out with a loud voice, and stopped their ears, and ran upon [Stephen] with one accord, and cast him out of the city, and stoned him. . . . and they stoned Stephen, [who was] calling upon God and saying, "Lord Jesus, receive my spirit" (Acts 7:57-59).

Occasionally such martyrdom is still required today. I was a freshman in college when five young men were brutally murdered by the Auca Indians in Ecuador. Although that event occurred more than thirty years ago, I can still remember where I was when I heard the news. Later I had the privilege of meeting the widow of Nate Saint, one of the men who was murdered. I determined at that time I was going to name a son Nathan.

Since then I have met many other Nathans who were named for that same young missionary. I have also met many people who are on the mission field today because they were touched by the lives and the deaths of those young men. God does allow bad things to happen to good people, but He also uses those events for His honor and glory.

The Old Testament recounts the interaction between God and Satan concerning Job:

> And the Lord said unto Satan, Hast thou considered my servant Job, that there is none like him in the earth, a perfect and an upright man, one that feareth God, and escheweth evil? Then Satan answered the Lord, and said, Doth Job fear God for nought? Hast thou not made an hedge about him, and about his house, and about all that he hath on every side? Thou hast blessed the work of his hands, and his substance is increased in the land. But put forth thine hand now, and touch all that he hath, and he

will curse thee to thy face. And the Lord said unto Satan, Behold, all that he hath is in thy power; only upon himself put not forth thine hand (Job 1:8-12).

Most of us are familiar with how Job lost all his possessions, his family and his health, but he remained true to God. Job was a good man, a God-fearing man, who experienced lots of trouble. I have often imagined a similar conversation between God and Satan concerning God's servant Marilyn. I pray that God can be as confident of me and of you as He was of His servant Job.

Decisions and Consequences

The God of Scripture allows good people to make wrong decisions and pay the consequences. Although God forgave David for his sin of adultery with Bathsheba, David still suffered great pain because of his sin:

And David said unto Nathan, I have sinned against the Lord. And Nathan said unto David, The Lord also hath put away thy sin; thou shalt not die. Howbeit, because by this deed thou hast given great occasion to the enemies of the Lord to blaspheme, the child also that is born unto thee shall surely die (2 Samuel 12:13,14).

In recent years we have seen many Christian leaders fall because of adultery and other immoral acts. Some have admitted their guilt, borne the consequences and gone on to serve God. Others have refused to admit their guilt, and they continue to embarrass the Christian community and defame the name of Christ. The God of Scripture is willing to forgive us, allow us to pay the price, and continue to use us, but it is apparent He will not tolerate unrepentance. We only dig a deeper hole for ourselves when we refuse to confess our sins.

In the book of Numbers we read that even though Moses was a great leader and feared God, at one time he chose to disobey God's instructions and thus missed his long awaited dream of going into the promised land (Numbers 20).

Evil People Affect Good People

The God of Scripture allows evil people to make decisions which will affect righteous people in seemingly unfair ways. Joseph was sold into slavery because of his brothers' jealousy. While in Egypt, he was wrongly accused and spent many years in prison. Even after all the cruel treatment and the injustices of his situation, he recognized this was all part of God's plan. He stated to his brothers, "Now therefore be not grieved, nor angry with yourselves, that ye sold me hither: for God did send me before you to preserve life. . . . But as for you, ye thought evil against me; but God meant it unto good, to bring to pass, as it is this day, to save much people alive" (Genesis 45:5; 50:20).

John the Baptist was killed on the whim of a guilt-ridden woman:

> But when Herod's birthday was kept, the daughter of Herodias danced before them, and pleased Herod. Whereupon he promised with an oath to give her whatsoever she would ask. And she, being before instructed of her mother, said, Give me here John the Baptist's head in a charger. And the king was sorry: nevertheless for the oath's sake, and them which sat with him at meat, he commanded it to be given her. And he sent, and beheaded John in the prison. And his head was brought in a charger, and given to the damsel: and she brought it to her mother (Matthew 14:6-11).

Unlikely Candidates

That same God of Scripture chose unlikely, undeserving people to accomplish great things and be lifted up to high places. David was a keeper of sheep when God chose him to be king of Israel. Daniel was one of many captives in Babylon, but God singled him out to be appointed chief president by King Darius.

Through the ages the God of Scripture has patiently wooed nations and individuals into a relationship with Himself even when they persistently disobeyed and turned their backs on Him. The Old Testament is full of examples of God's frustration with Israel, yet He continued to protect and preserve them as His chosen people.

When Jonah refused to obey God's command to warn the city of Ninevah about their pending destruction, God pursued him even into the belly of a large fish. Although God insisted on Jonah's obedience, He was still patient with him when Jonah chose to pout for a while.

In the New Testament, God persistently pursued Saul even though he continued to systematically annihilate the Christians. Eventually he bowed in submission to Jesus Christ. He then changed his name to Paul and God used him to write a major portion of the New Testament.

The complete picture of the God of Scripture also has to include the fact that He willingly gave His Son as a living sacrifice for every individual when we did nothing to deserve such a gift of love.

Where Is God When I Hurt?

Most of us are willing to accept God's attributes of love, mercy and forgiveness, but there are parts of God's being that are sometimes difficult to understand. We want to ignore His attributes of judgment, discipline and order. He also allows us to live in a world where everyone has freedom of choice, good or bad.

Recently I heard John Ramey, pastor of River City Christian Fellowship in Sacramento, share what our approach should be when trouble comes: "We need to ask why in faith — knowing God has the answer." Usually our whys come in the form of "Why me?" "Why isn't God paying attention?" Pastor John pointed out that it's okay to ask why in confidence, knowing full well that God does have the answer.

I equate our asking why in an appropriate way to someone who is a passenger in a car. The passenger may ask the driver, "Why did we turn here?" even though the passenger knows the driver has the road map and is confident the driver knows why he turned at a certain point. Likewise, it is acceptable for us to ask God, "Why did we turn here?" because we have total confidence that God has the road map and He knows where He is taking us.

When the angel told Zacharias that his wife would conceive a child, Zacharias responded, "But this is impossible! I'm an old man now, and my wife is also well along in years" (Luke 1:18, TLB). He doubted that God knew what He was doing or was capable of carrying out His prophesied plan. The angel responded,

> I am Gabriel! I stand in the very presence of God. It was he who sent me to you with this good news! And now, because you haven't believed me, you are to be stricken silent, unable to speak until the child is born. For my words will certainly come true at the proper time (Luke 1:19,20, TLB).

It is very clear that God and Gabriel were not pleased with Zacharias's doubting attitude.

Pastor John points out that it is all right to ask how or why if we are asking for information and insight rather than asking in disbelief. The story in Luke continues:

> The following month God sent the angel Gabriel to Nazareth, a village in Galilee, to a virgin, Mary, engaged to be married to a man named Joseph, a descendant of King David. Gabriel appeared to her and said, "Congratulations, favored lady! The Lord is with you!" Con-

fused and disturbed, Mary tried to think what the angel
could mean. "Don't be frightened, Mary," the angel told
her, "for God has decided to wonderfully bless you! Very
soon now, you will become pregnant and have a baby boy,
and you are to name him 'Jesus.' He shall be very great
and shall be called the Son of God. And the Lord God shall
give him the throne of his ancestor David. And he shall
reign over Israel forever; his Kingdom shall never end!"
Mary asked the angel, "But how can I have a baby? I am
a virgin." The angel replied, "The Holy Spirit shall come
upon you, and the power of God shall overshadow you;
so the baby born to you will be utterly holy — the Son of
God." . . . Mary said, "I am the Lord's servant, and I am
willing to do whatever he wants. May everything you said
come true" (Luke 1:26-37, TLB).

Mary had lots of questions, but she was confident
God had all of the answers and she was willing to follow His
instructions.

Pastor John makes the point that when we are not
open to God's plan we are vulnerable to difficulties in our
Christian walk. He states that first comes the trial and, if
we are not grounded in God's Word, confusion will come.
"How could God allow this? What is He doing?" After confusion will come spiritual relaxation: "What difference does
it make that I'm a Christian? Why should I serve a God who
has failed me and let me down?" Then our spiritual life will
suffer. We will go through the motions, but we will experience little satisfaction or reality. The next step will
likely be to leave God and enter a state of apostasy.

On the other hand, I've found that the opposite can
also be true. When a trial comes, we take that first step of
faith and believe God has a plan even if it doesn't make
sense to us. Confusion begins to resolve and we have confidence within our trauma even if we don't understand why
it is happening. Instead of spiritual relaxation, we develop
a spiritual zeal and awareness that we may never have had

before. We become attuned to God's voice. A spiritual reality sets in that brings with it a peace and a calm in spite of the troubles brewing around us.

Does that mean we should never ask questions or that we are weak if we ever entertain doubts? Absolutely not. I feel uncomfortable around people who just accept what happens to them with nothing more than a nod. We grow strong as we wrestle with spiritual truths. Our confidence comes from asking questions, searching Scripture, confronting God in prayer, and acquiring answers that satisfy the hunger in our hearts.

When I first met Katherine, she believed she came from an ideal Christian home. But she couldn't understand why she had such a poor self-image, wrestled with unexplained anger, did not deal well with sexual issues, was anorexic, was often severely depressed, and had even considered suicide. Katherine knew she had received Christ as her Savior, but she did not feel close to God, and she had trouble trusting God or anyone else.

Through nearly three years of intensive therapy, Katherine has been able to release the blocked memories of her childhood. She now knows she was molested by several family members from the time she was two, continuing into her early teens. Katherine and I have talked together, cried together, and even asked, "Why?" together.

Katherine has not been content to learn about herself; she has made a concerted effort to get to know her God better at the same time. I have seen her hit the very depths of pain and suffering, but I have also seen her become strong in her faith and become determined to use these awful experiences to help others. She is not willing to let her pain be wasted.

I have learned that our healing will begin when "God, *why* is this happening to me?" turns to "God, *what* do you want me to do with this situation?"

Pastor John had these concluding thoughts: "The greater the odds are against you, the more important you are to God in that situation. Noah lived against tremendous odds, and it mattered tremendously that he was willing to hang in there."

How about you? Have you felt totally alone in your suffering? Through my own experience and the testimony of others, I can confidently say, try the God of Scripture. Get to know Him. He is the dream maker, the dream breaker, and the dream remaker. He won't fail you. He will give you the strength to dream again. Launch out to God.

Questions to Ask Yourself

When I experienced the death of my dream, what surprised me most about God?

Upon what had I based my expectation of God? (Scripture, teaching at your church, other Christians, family beliefs, other)

Spend much time searching Scripture yourself to make sure your understanding of God is scripturally based.

As you have time to re-evaluate God, list the new characteristics you have discovered from Scripture.

Can you now better reconcile the death of your dream with the God of Scripture?

6

Launching Out in Trust

The dictionary defines trust as "a confident reliance on the integrity, honesty, or justice of another; faith." Children of alcoholics, and victims of divorce, adultery, molestation, physical or emotional abuse, rape and other violent crimes experience a breaking of trust. Those who have been betrayed by someone who misused a confidence, someone who exploited them in a personal or business relationship, or someone who violated the family standards also understand the breaking of trust. Trust can be breached by an institution such as the government, the justice system, or the medical or legal profession as well.

Oswald Chambers observes:

> If I put my trust in human beings first, I will end in despairing of everyone; I will become bitter, because I have insisted on man being what no man ever can be— absolutely right. Never trust anything but the grace of God in yourself or in anyone else.[1]

Chronic Distrust Syndrome

Recently Dr. Larry Poland, author of *The Coming Persecution,* spoke on "The Inability to Trust." He stated:

All of living is built on trust. Thousands of times a day we place our trust in various things which we feel are deserving of our trust. In so doing, we continually "risk our lives."

A frightening epidemic is sweeping modern day America. This epidemic is threatening to destroy the spiritual, emotional and physical strength of our nation. The epidemic is the inability to trust. I call it "chronic distrust syndrome."

Dr. Poland listed the marks of chronic distrust:

- A personal insecurity accompanied by high anxiety or gripping fear.
- The inability to establish deep, meaningful relationships.
- Instability in all areas of life involving relationships (marriage, job, team efforts, etc.).
- A tendency to relate to others on a superficial basis and to "run" when the relationship gets to the stage where it requires commitment or "surrender" to the other in trust.
- A desperate need to be in control in relationships.
- A cynical approach to life, to others, to authorities and to God.
- The inability to establish a strong Christian walk and experience spiritual power.

Dr. Poland points out that without trust one can never please God nor serve Him. "And without faith it is impossible to please God, because anyone who comes to him must believe that he exists and that he rewards those who earnestly seek him" (Hebrews 11:6).

Without trust one can never receive the blessings God has for His own:

> But when he asks, he must believe and not doubt, because he who doubts is like a wave of the sea, blown and tossed by the wind. That man should not think he will receive anything from the Lord; he is a double-minded man, unstable in all he does (James 1:6-8).

Without trust one can never really have security and stability:

> This is what the Lord says: "Cursed is the one who trusts in man, who depends on flesh for his strength and whose heart turns away from the Lord. He will be like a bush in the wastelands; he will not see prosperity when it comes. He will dwell in the parched places of the desert, in a salt land where no one lives. But blessed is the man who trusts in the Lord, whose confidence is in him. He will be like a tree planted by the water that sends out its roots by the stream. It does not fear when heat comes; its leaves are always green. It has no worries in a year of drought and never fails to bear fruit" (Jeremiah 17:5-8).

No one can ever really love without trusting:

> God is love. Whosoever lives in love lives in God, and God in him. Love is made complete among us so that we will have confidence on the day of judgment, because in this world we are like him. There is no fear in love. But perfect love drives out fear, because fear has to do with punishment. The man who fears is not made perfect in love (1 John 4:16b-18).

Oswald Chambers writes:

> It is not our trust that keeps us, but the God in whom we trust who keeps us. We are always in danger of trusting in our trust, believing in our belief, having faith in our faith. All these things can be shaken; we have to base our faith on those things which cannot be shaken.[2]

Developing an Attitude of Trust

Dr. Poland has five suggestions on how to learn to trust God:

1. Establish a separate category for God that distinguishes Him from human beings in your thinking.

"God is not a man, that he should lie, nor a son of man, that he should change his mind. Does he speak and then not act? Does he promise and not fulfill? I have received a command to bless; he has blessed, and I cannot change it" (Numbers 23:19,20).

Since hearing Dr. Poland's message, I have experimented with using names other than "Father" for God when I address Him in prayer. There are many names we can use: King, Lord, Shepherd, Counselor, Friend, Leader, Savior, Master. If the father image of God is difficult for you, try using one of His other names. It will make a difference in your attitude toward Him. I didn't have any particular problem with using "Father," but I did enjoy using other names. I think "King" and "Your Majesty" paint my favorite picture of God. I could see myself entering the royal hall and bowing in His presence.

Dick Purnell has written an excellent little workbook on this subject, *Knowing God By His Names*,[3] which I highly recommend.

2. Submit to the command to trust God as an act of the will rather than relying on your feelings.

"Do not let your hearts be troubled. Trust in God, trust also in me" (John 14:1).

Trusting in God takes an act of our will. It is believing something will happen before it happens. I can trust God to help me be kind to a person I do not like, but then I must approach that person with the intention and determination to be kind. I can trust God to help me not be fearful in a fear-producing situation, and then I must do what I can to alleviate those fears.

Since Nathan's death I often become fearful if a family member is late in arriving home. Recently I called my son's home and no one answered. I called again later in the evening and still there was no answer. It was time to go to bed and I had a choice to make. I could trust God to take care of my children and I could go to bed and sleep. Or I could sit up and worry until I reached my son by phone. I chose to go to bed.

Going to bed wasn't too hard, but sleeping was another story. I prayed that God would protect my family, then I prayed that Satan would be bound in this situation. I quoted Bible verses until I fell asleep. I chose to trust God, and He gave me the power to follow through on that choice.

3. Ask the Holy Spirit to control you, producing trust.

"But the fruit of the Spirit is love, joy, peace, patience, kindness, goodness, faithfulness" (Galatians 5:22).

As we yield our lives to the Holy Spirit, He will produce the proper fruit in us that will help us build our trust in Him and in His faithfulness.

4. Learn to trust God as a "back up" to trusting others.

"It is better to take refuge in the Lord than to put confidence in man" (Psalm 118:8, RSV).

In the last few years in the Christian world, we have seen what happens when we fix our eyes on people rather than on Christ. We must realize that no person has the ability to never let us down. No one is a perfect human being. When human trust is broken, we need to place our ultimate trust in God because He is the only one who is 100 percent trustworthy.

5. Practice extending the boundaries of your trust in small but consistent increments.

"The fear of man lays a snare, but he who trusts in the Lord is safe" (Proverbs 29:25, RSV).

As we are trying to rebuild our trust in God and in mankind, it is important that we put ourselves in vulnerable situations. As Dr. Poland suggests, we may want to extend the boundaries a little at a time. Start by trusting a friend with some of your feelings or by sharing a little of your story. If the friend is understanding and responsive, share a little more. If the friend reproves you or laughs at you, you have a choice to make on how you will react. You could decide never to share a confidence with anyone again. Or you could decide to try another friend. I hope you will try the latter.

When Wayne was suddenly unemployed, he chose to trust some of his closest friends with his situation and his feelings. He writes:

> My close friends provided a wonderful safety net. Six people—Bruce, Dan, Marilyn, Grace, Margaret and Chuck—all kept in close touch and seemed to call at just the time when I needed their insight or help. I am a person who had felt that friends were not that important— I would opt to go through tough times alone.
>
> But during this episode in my life, I learned the true value of loving, caring friends, and I accepted their help, advice and support. They helped me to make accurate evaluations of myself. They let me air my feelings of frustration without passing judgment or providing from-the-hip recommendations. They quoted scripture as it applied to their lives, not as an easy way out of a difficult situation. They affirmed my self-worth which had slipped

a good deal. They took my wife and me out to dinner when they knew we needed a change of scenery. Their closeness changed my life and my perspective.

Learning to Trust Again

If you are one who has experienced the death of a dream because people have failed you, such as in divorce, abuse, a broken relationship, or a bad business venture, you will probably be hesitant to trust again. Learn about yourself before you get involved in a similar relationship again. Study the "Personality Profile" and the "Spiritual Gifts Inventory" which are presented later in this section. Find out what your innate and God-given abilities are. Spend a lot of time journalizing. See if there are any clues as to why the previous situation did not go well.

If your trust was broken by an institution or system, you will probably have to realize that the system may never change. My husband and I were very disappointed in the judicial process as we watched the handling of the manslaughter case after Nathan's death. We soon realized that the victim and the victim's family have very little representation within our present criminal justice system. I believe I could still work with a district attorney's office, and even trust the prosecutor, but my expectations would be different.

As you get to know yourself better and understand your own thoughts and feelings about your situation, you will learn to trust your own judgment again. That is the first step in being able to trust others—trusting yourself. As you gain confidence in your own judgment, you can give yourself permission not to trust untrustworthy people. When we do not have confidence in ourselves, we chastise ourselves whenever we doubt others. It really is all right to make a conscious decision not to trust someone if they have proven themselves untrustworthy.

Finally, we need to practice trusting: "Today I am going to answer Nancy honestly when she asks how I am feeling. I am going to tell her some of the emotional battles I am facing."

After you have launched out in trust, even the tiniest bit, give yourself an evaluation. If it went well, praise yourself for your success. If it didn't go well, praise yourself for the attempt and think about how you would do it differently next time. Then plan what exercise in trust you are going to launch next.

By the time you have finished reading the "Launching Out" section, it is my prayer that you will be willing to trust God again and through your trust in Him you will be able to trust others again, one at a time.

"Trust in him at all times, O people; pour out your heart before him; God is a refuge for us" (Psalm 62:8, RSV).

Questions to Ask Yourself

If you do not have confidence or trust in yourself, do you know why?

List ways you can help yourself and include counseling in that list if trusting seems to be a chronic problem.

In which areas do you have the most difficulty trusting God? (salvation, security of salvation, personal safety, family's safety, health, spouse, other)

Search the Scriptures to find verses you can memorize and quote when doubts about the above areas come in.

Name someone you want to learn to trust and list ways you can launch out in that area.

7

Launching Out in Prayer

So often when we are in trouble, it's only after we have tried every possible solution that we say, "I guess there's nothing left to do except pray." Our attitude needs to be reversed. Prayer should be the *first* thing we do in any situation.

Prayer is our way of speaking with God directly. Unfortunately, that may be part of the reason we don't consider prayer our first course of action in a difficult situation. When trouble comes, when things aren't going the way we planned, often the last person we want to talk with is God. We're not sure we can trust Him. We may feel He let us down. However, the best way to get things straightened out with God is to keep talking with Him even when we don't understand His ways.

In *December's Song* I share the story of the traumatic birth of our first grandchild, Katherine Naté. For several days we did not know if she would live or die. The first evening after her birth I stood numbly peering through the glass into the Neonatal Intensive Care Unit where my son Matthew was tenderly stroking Kate's tiny little frame. A woman standing next to me started a conversation. Her child was in the same unit because of a difficult birth, but her little boy was now out of danger. She told me she was a Christian and believed her child's recovery was an answer to prayer.

All day I had tried to pray, but no words would come out. I couldn't gather my thoughts enough to pray and, frankly, I wasn't too sure how I felt about God or if prayer did any good anyway. I asked this young mother, "How did you pray? What did you ask for?"

She answered, "Oh, honey, I just prayed for mercy. Whatever would be merciful—to let my child live or to let him die. That's what I wanted."

Then she added, "I'll pray for mercy for your Kate."

I muttered a weak "Thank you," but I really wasn't sure if prayer would help much.

Glen and I left Matthew and little Kate about 2 A.M. to drive home to San Bernardino where I washed, dried and packed some clothes while Glen caught a quick nap. About 6 A.M. we headed back to San Diego feeling weary and discouraged. It was our twenty-ninth wedding anniversary, but there didn't seem to be much to celebrate. Our granddaughter was clinging to life by a thread; we could possibly be attending a funeral within the next few days. Life seemed to take too much effort.

I wearily reached over and picked up a Bible which was laying on the car seat next to me. I don't really believe in the "hunt and peck" system of reading Scripture, but that day I basically dared God to give me a verse which would comfort me and I let the pages just drop open.

My eyes fell on Psalm 103 and I absentmindedly read until I came to verse 17: "But the mercy of the Lord is from everlasting to everlasting upon them that fear him, and his righteousness unto children's children." I focused on the words *mercy* and *children's children*. God was promising everlasting mercy to me and to my children's children — my Kate!

It was still many days before we knew Kate would live and many more months beyond that before we were certain there wasn't permanent brain damage, but during that time I was able to pray. God and I were on speaking terms again, and I could trust Him to show mercy to me and my family.

Making a Pattern of Prayer

As you walked through the death of your dream, you may have felt frustrated when you tried to pray. That's all right. As you start to launch out into life again, though, I encourage you to get back into a pattern of prayer.

A few years ago a friend shared with me that he had started writing out his prayers and had found it a tremendous blessing in his time with the Lord. Since that time I, too, have been writing my prayers to the Lord. When you are working through a trauma, writing out prayers can be especially meaningful and beneficial.

Buy yourself a notebook and keep it in a private place. You may want to divide your notebook into sections for different types of prayer: praise to God, petitions for yourself, your family, and your friends, etc. I have a section where I share my deepest desires and dreams. I also have a section where I am quiet before the Lord. I listen to what He has to say to me, and I write down those thoughts and instructions as they come to my mind. I date each entry so I can look back and see what the Lord has done in my life in recent months or years.

Oswald Chambers wrote:

> A most beneficial exercise in secret prayer before the Father is to write things down so that I see exactly what I think and want to say. Only those who have tried

these ways know the ineffable benefit of such strenuous times in secret.[1]

Prayer can happen at any place and anytime. My husband and I go to a health club three mornings a week. I spend twenty-five minutes on a stationary bicycle, and I use that time to pray. I walk out of the gym feeling physically and spiritually invigorated.

Again quoting Oswald Chambers: "There is always a suitable place to pray, to lift up your eyes to God; there is no need to get to a place of prayer, pray wherever you are."[2]

As we work on establishing a stronger relationship with God, He will supply us with the wisdom and power to renew and nurture our relationships with those around us. We will also gain the strength we need to launch out and face life without our dream.

> In my distress I called upon the Lord, and cried unto my God: he heard my voice out of his temple, and my cry came before him, even into his ears (Psalm 18:6, KJV).

Questions to Ask Yourself

Do you now have a daily prayer time?

Is it fulfilling?

What seems to be missing?

Take time now to write in a notebook and tell God how you feel about your present prayer life. Share with Him how you would like it to be. Share with God how you are feeling right now.

Sit quietly and ask God to speak to you. Write down any thoughts as they come to your mind.

8

Launching Out in Truth

Part of launching out after the death of a dream is knowing and accepting the truth about ourselves, about others and about our dreams. Many professionals have discovered that an effective tool for facing the truth about ourselves is *journalizing*.

Journalizing is not the same as keeping a diary of events or daily happenings. It is not the same as writing a prayer journal of conversations with God. Journalizing is recording feelings. You write about the emotional impact of events rather than simply recording the occurrence of events.

Florence Littauer says, "To journalize is to think, planning today to make mental pictures for the future."[1]

Journalizing methods can be simple or complicated, depending on what's comfortable for you. You can write in a notebook, use a typewriter or computer, or talk your thoughts into a tape recorder. If you don't know what to start writing about, I'd suggest you refer to the inventory section of Fred and Florence Littauer's book, *Freeing Your Mind From Memories That Bind* or Florence Littauer's book, *It Takes So Little to Be Above Average*. Set aside a few pages in your journal for childhood events, family background, hometown memories, and perhaps several pages for each one of your children.

Exodus 17:14 states: "Write this into a permanent record to be remembered forever" (TLB).

As we record our feelings close to the time that they occur, we will preserve those feelings forever. Shortly after Nathan's death I made this entry in my journal:

> The fog still hasn't lifted. I move, I walk, I talk, but it is all automatic. There is little feeling. Sometimes the fog lifts and the feelings rush in. Then all I can do is cry. It seems the only time I am real, reacting honestly, without guarding every word or look, I start to cry.
>
> When the fog lifts for a brief moment, it is as though someone just kicked me in the stomach. As I am reeling with the pain, my mind registers the one prevailing thought: Nathan is gone; NATHAN IS GONE. When I can't stand the pain anymore, my mind goes back into neutral, back into the fog.

It would be hard for me now to accurately describe how I felt the first few months after Nathan's death if I hadn't kept the journal. I realize now how important it is to be able to recall those feelings. I am able to help other grievers because I can still identify with their pain and show them my own progression through pain and healing. Since they can identify with the pain I felt at the early stages of grief, they become more apt to believe that healing will come for them, as it has for me, as they move along in their own grief process.

Honest journalizing reveals the truth about what has happened to us and our feelings about those events. It may also reveal unresolved issues or areas where God needs to do more work. Unforgiveness in my heart showed up in my writing. I realized I was often using words such as *angry, hurt* and *betrayed* when I wrote. As I responded to God's prompting and forgave those who had hurt me, my use of these words decreased.

Knowing Where We Are Going

The only way in which a truth can become of vital interest to me is when I am brought into the place where that truth is needed.[2]

If our true feelings are recorded and preserved, we will be able to look through our journal and allow the Holy Spirit to reveal spiritual and personal needs in our lives. We will also be able to recognize personal victories and growth as the pieces come together in His perfect timing.

While Wayne was between jobs, he spent a lot of time journalizing:

> Time in my journal proved to me that God knew what He was doing. I cried out to the Lord in my journal and He answered me with great swiftness.
>
> I spent time evaluating myself. I knew my strengths and weaknesses, but what did I want to do? Did I want to work for someone else again? Did I want to start my own business? I didn't know. Together the Lord and I wrestled with these questions in my journal. Eventually He showed me exactly what I was to do. I don't think I ever would have had the kind of insight I needed without the journal.
>
> I can remember many days when my wife and I both were stretched to our limits because of the pressure. At those moments, it was so refreshing to be able to pick up our journals and spend time with the Lord. We renewed our relationship with God and began to see His healing and feel His touch.

An additional tool to help us discover the truth about ourselves is counseling. We should not be afraid to go to a professional or lay counselor, but we do need to be wise in choosing one. The best way to find a good counselor is through the referral of a satisfied client. If you have no such referral, don't hesitate to call various counselors and ask specific questions regarding their specialty areas. If you do not see some specific progress within the first few months with a counselor, feel free to change.

Whether you choose to journalize, seek counseling, or both, make it a priority to know the truth about yourself and about God.

There is no one in the world more easy to get to than God. Only one thing prevents us from getting there, and that is the refusal to tell ourselves the truth.[3]

Questions to Ask Yourself

Try journalizing for at least one month. Which method will you use? (notebook, computer, tape recorder, etc.)

Notice certain words that keep appearing in your writings. Make a list of them. What do you think God is trying to reveal to you through the repetition of these words? What action does He want you to take?

9

Launching Out Emotionally

After we have let go of our dreams, our unforgiveness, and our grief, we may feel somewhat stripped of the emotional and spiritual drive that once motivated us. We may feel that we'll never have the emotional energy to move past our broken dreams and live again.

Let me assure you, those feelings are perfectly normal. It's important to allow yourself a "cooling-down" time, a neutral period where you don't have to make any major, life-changing decisions. We need to use this time to get to know ourselves again. Some are facing life as single people after many years of marriage. Others are childless even though they gave birth to children. Some have lost their wealth and are using words like *budget, bankruptcy* and *foreclosure*. Others are trying to adjust to a body that now requires special medical attention. Many are facing truths about themselves and their families which have been hidden for years.

During this cooling-down time, which I recommend should be a minimum of one year, I encourage you to ask yourself some questions: What are my God-given abilities? How have I changed because of the death of my dream? What would I like to do now?

God-given Abilities

After the death of a dream, we need to take stock of our assets, our talents, our training and our God-given abilities. Sometimes when you're really down it's hard to think of anything positive about yourself or your abilities.

For awhile after Nathan's death I didn't think I was capable of doing anything. I didn't feel worth very much. I was no longer known as Nate's mom; my identity seemed to have died with him. But as I worked through the grief process, I realized I was not just Nate's, Matthew's or Mellyn's mom or Glen's wife. I had to discover who I was as Marilyn Willett Heavilin. Who did God create her to be?

One of the things that helped me so much as I got to know myself was learning about the temperaments or personality types. There are many different tests you can take to discover your temperament. The one I am including in this book was written by Fred Littauer and is used in many of Florence Littauer's books. There are four basic temperament types: Sanguine, Choleric, Melancholy and Phlegmatic. On the next few pages I've described the traits each temperament is likely to have.[1]

Sanguine

Obvious Needs:	fun and excitement
Underlying Need:	constant encouragement and approval
Emotions:	childlike, changeable, intense but temporary
Anger:	quick, short-lived temper
Reactions to Grief:	may display superficial joy; may try to make people laugh or crack jokes that seem in poor taste; has strong denial system – "Everything is fine"

Spiritual Struggles: struggles with lust: food, clothes, wealth, sex; need for immediate gratification; hard to comprehend God's holiness—everything must be fun and free of restrictions; needs lots of spiritual excitement; makes great commitments with little follow-through

Work Strengths: volunteers for jobs; thinks up new activities; looks great on the surface; creative and colorful; has energy and enthusiasm; starts in a flashy way; inspires others to join; charms others to work

Work Weaknesses: would rather talk than work; forgets obligations; doesn't follow through; confidence fades fast; undisciplined; priorities out of order; decides by feelings; easily distracted; wastes time talking[1]

The Sanguines are the life of the party. They love excitement and change. They will be full of wonderful ideas, but they need someone else to follow through and complete their ideas. They thrive on verbal compliments and public praise.

Choleric

Obvious Needs: control and productivity

Underlying Need: appreciation for responsible and dutiful endeavors

Emotions: underdeveloped; won't show emotion for fear of losing control

Anger: logic-based anger rooted in impatience; verbally destructive anger; shows anger instead of sadness; often unable to say, "I'm sorry"

Reactions to Grief:	anger against God; very little emotion; may bury himself in work or other activity; strongest denial system: "It's over—let's get on with life"
Spiritual Struggles:	battles with lack of tenderness; struggles with God's sovereignty
Work Strengths:	goal oriented; sees the whole picture; organizes well; seeks practical solutions; moves quickly to action; delegates work; insists on production; makes the goal; stimulates activity; thrives on opposition
Work Weaknesses:	little tolerance for mistakes; doesn't analyze details; bored by trivia; may make rash decisions; may be rude or tactless; manipulates people; demanding of others; work may become a god; expects complete loyalty in the ranks[2]

When it comes to work, efficiency and productivity, the Choleric is a powerhouse. Cholerics measure their lives by their accomplishments and tend to dismiss any who are not as productive. They will rise to the top professionally and will produce goal-oriented families. The biggest difficulty for cholerics is to allow room for emotions and expressions of feelings. To them, showing emotion signifies weakness, and cholerics are anything but weak.

Melancholy

Obvious Needs:	perfection and sensitivity
Underlying Need:	creative tenderness
Emotions:	intense sensitivity; medium highs, low lows; hurt if people don't respond to his needs

Anger: "green stamp collector," meaning he'll collect little wrongs done to him and keep the anger inside until the final hurt (last green stamp), which causes tremendous rage

Reactions to Grief: deep depression; angry at injustice; guilt; can't let go

Spiritual Struggles: unwisely self-sacrificing; becomes overextended and overwhelmed; struggles with grace – wants to repay God; has problems receiving from others; has trouble balancing faith and service; difficult to let others minister to him; may become spiritually critical

Work Strengths: schedule oriented; perfectionist; high standards; detail conscious; persistent and thorough; orderly and organized; neat and tidy; economical; sees problems and finds creative solutions; desires to finish what he starts; likes charts, graphs, figures, lists

Work Weaknesses: not people oriented; depressed over imperfections; chooses difficult work; hesitant to start projects; spends too much time planning; prefers analysis to work; self-deprecating; hard to please; standards often too high; deep need for approval[3]

Melancholies thrive on deep emotions and deep thoughts. They are sensitive to others' needs and are also hurt easily. They are organized and get depressed when things get out of order. They tend to become overworked because they are afraid to say no to others' requests.

Phlegmatic

Obvious Needs: peace and quiet

Underlying Need: a sense of value as a person

Emotions: feels emotion but can't display it; fear of conflict; goes blank in confrontation

Anger: responds to anger with sadness; anger may come out in sarcasm

Reactions to Grief: shows little emotion; can't express feelings verbally; becomes withdrawn and more critical

Spiritual Struggles: wrestles with servanthood because of laziness; difficult to accept God as absolute truth; shirks spiritual responsibilities; tends to be self-righteous; may seem unapproachable

Work Strengths: competent and steady; peaceful and agreeable; has administrative ability; mediates problems; avoids conflicts; good under pressure; finds the easy way

Work Weaknesses: not goal oriented; lacks self-motivation; hard to get moving; resents being pushed; lazy and careless; discourages others; would rather watch[4]

One of the Phlegmatics' best traits is dependability. They don't really like change and they appreciate routine. They do not like confrontation and often their motto is, "Don't rock the boat." Phlegmatics seldom have enemies and can make good leaders because of their adaptability and peacemaking ability.

Expect Change

I've discovered that after a major trauma, our temperaments may go through a radical change.

When I first took the personality profile in my early thirties, the test came out pretty well balanced between Choleric and Melancholy. That was probably quite accurate. I did not take the test again until about a year and a half after Nathan died. When I took the temperament test at one of Florence Littauer's C.L.A.S.S. sessions (Christian Leaders, Artists and Speakers Seminars), I couldn't believe it. The results showed an almost even balance of Melancholy and Sanguine. That is not me at all. I went to one of the C.L.A.S.S. staff right away and asked, "What's wrong with me?"

She said, "Marilyn, you just buried a son a year and a half ago. You are trying to discover yourself again."

Being a Choleric, I had reacted strongly to the fact that I had lost all control over Nathan's death and the events that followed. The insurance settlement dragged on and on. We had to go through a manslaughter trial which meant I didn't have control of scheduling my own calendar. The District Attorney told me when I had to be in town and when I could leave. I couldn't control the outcome of the trial. If I were controlling it, the man would have been convicted quickly; but the final decision took more than fifteen months to reach and he got off on a plea bargain.

I began to understand why the Choleric part of my personality had retreated. I knew I could not control the events around me, so I pulled back and didn't try.

My friend suggested I pray for God's guidance and just "take it slow." She said I should watch and see if the real me didn't eventually emerge. A year or so later, when I was taking the training for Philippian Ministries, I took the test again. I was so excited because the results showed

Melancholy/Choleric. My temperament is more Melancholy than it was before, and I would agree that is quite accurate. After you've gone through what I've gone through in the last twenty years, it is bound to affect you. Indeed, I hope it has. The Choleric has tamed down a little bit and the Melancholy's sensitive response to other people has risen.

These are the kinds of things we need to evaluate when we are ready to move on after a crisis. Who am I? What temperament do I have?

Evaluating Strengths and Weaknesses

Then I asked myself, "What would a Melancholy person like to do?" Melancholies are very sensitive; they like to help people. They sense needs where others might not. The Melancholy in me likes to work alone on things. I am quite content to work in my office all day and it's fine with me if the phone doesn't ring and no one comes by. The Choleric likes to have control. If I have a job to do, the Choleric part says, "Get it done" and the Melancholy part says, "Get it done right." I am learning to understand what I require of myself. You still have time regardless of your age to learn these things about yourself and it will bring so much peace as your understanding grows.

It's helpful to make a list of your personality strengths and weaknesses. My personal strengths and weaknesses list looks like this:

Strengths

Goal oriented

Moves quickly to action

Schedule oriented

Detail conscious

Economical

Organizes well

Insists on production

High standards

Orderly and organized

Need to finish what I start

Weaknesses

Little tolerance for mistakes	Doesn't analyze details
May be rude or tactless	Demanding of others
Demands loyalty in the ranks	Depressed over imperfections
Chooses difficult work	Hesitant to start projects
Hard to please	Deep need for approval

Take some time to evaluate yourself on your own strengths and weaknesses. You'll be providing valuable insight into who you are as a person and what you are capable of doing.

My friend Jan went through a severe trauma in her marriage. The marital trust was broken and Jan questioned whether their marriage could be saved. In the midst of the trauma Jan attended a seminar where Florence Littauer spoke on the temperaments.

Jan writes: "I firmly believe the best tool for my husband and me in rebuilding our dreams has been understanding the personality temperaments. I am a Melancholy with a smattering of Choleric and my husband is a Phlegmatic. I began to appreciate his sense of humor. I understood his laid-back attitude so I began to relax and 'smell the roses' as he put it. We laugh more, and we love more."

Understanding the temperaments will help you, too. As you begin to appreciate your own God-given abilities, you'll be able to allow those around you to discover and appreciate their own uniqueness as well.

I urge you to take time now to fill out the "Personality Profile" which is provided for you on the following pages.*

---

* The "Personality Profile" is reprinted with permission from its author, Fred Littauer.

DIRECTIONS — In each of the following rows of four words across, place an X in front of the one word that most often applies to you. Continue through all forty lines. Be sure each number is marked. If you are not sure of which word "most applies", ask a spouse or a friend.

STRENGTHS

#				
1	___ Adventurous	___ Adaptable	___ Animated	___ Analytical
2	___ Persistent	___ Playful	___ Persuasive	___ Peaceful
3	___ Submissive	___ Self-sacrificing	___ Sociable	___ Strong-willed
4	___ Considerate	___ Controlled	___ Competitive	___ Convincing
5	___ Refreshing	___ Respectful	___ Reserved	___ Resourceful
6	___ Satisfied	___ Sensitive	___ Self-reliant	___ Spirited
7	___ Planner	___ Patient	___ Positive	___ Promoter
8	___ Sure	___ Spontaneous	___ Scheduled	___ Shy
9	___ Orderly	___ Obliging	___ Outspoken	___ Optimistic
10	___ Friendly	___ Faithful	___ Funny	___ Forceful
11	___ Daring	___ Delightful	___ Diplomatic	___ Detailed
12	___ Cheerful	___ Consistent	___ Cultured	___ Confident
13	___ Idealistic	___ Independent	___ Inoffensive	___ Inspiring
14	___ Demonstrative	___ Decisive	___ Dry humor	___ Deep
15	___ Mediator	___ Musical	___ Mover	___ Mixes easily
16	___ Thoughtful	___ Tenacious	___ Talker	___ Tolerant
17	___ Listener	___ Loyal	___ Leader	___ Lively
18	___ Contented	___ Chief	___ Chartmaker	___ Cute
19	___ Perfectionist	___ Pleasant	___ Productive	___ Popular
20	___ Bouncy	___ Bold	___ Behaved	___ Balanced

WEAKNESSES

21	___ Blank	___ Bashful	___ Brassy	___ Bossy
22	___ Undisciplined	___ Unsympathetic	___ Unenthusiastic	___ Unforgiving
23	___ Reticent	___ Resentful	___ Resistant	___ Repetitious
24	___ Fussy	___ Fearful	___ Forgetful	___ Frank
25	___ Impatient	___ Insecure	___ Indecisive	___ Interrupts
26	___ Unpopular	___ Uninvolved	___ Unpredictable	___ Unaffectionate
27	___ Headstrong	___ Haphazard	___ Hard to please	___ Hesitant
28	___ Plain	___ Pessimistic	___ Proud	___ Permissive
29	___ Angered easily	___ Aimless	___ Argumentative	___ Alienated
30	___ Naive	___ Negative attitude	___ Nervy	___ Nonchalant
31	___ Worrier	___ Withdrawn	___ Workaholic	___ Wants credit
32	___ Too sensitive	___ Tactless	___ Timid	___ Talkative
33	___ Doubtful	___ Disorganized	___ Domineering	___ Depressed
34	___ Inconsistent	___ Introvert	___ Intolerant	___ Indifferent
35	___ Messy	___ Moody	___ Mumbles	___ Manipulative
36	___ Slow	___ Stubborn	___ Show-off	___ Skeptical
37	___ Loner	___ Lord over	___ Lazy	___ Loud
38	___ Sluggish	___ Suspicious	___ Short-tempered	___ Scatterbrained
39	___ Revengeful	___ Restless	___ Reluctant	___ Rash
40	___ Compromising	___ Critical	___ Crafty	___ Changeable

NOW TRANSFER ALL YOUR X's TO THE CORRESPONDING WORDS ON THE PERSONALITY SCORING SHEET AND ADD UP YOUR TOTALS.

STRENGTHS

	SANGUINE POPULAR	CHOLERIC POWERFUL	MELANCHOLY PERFECT	PHLEGMATIC PEACEFUL
1	Animated	Adventurous	Analytical	Adaptable
2	Playful	Persuasive	Persistent	Peaceful
3	Sociable	Strong-willed	Self-sacrificing	Submissive
4	Convincing	Competitive	Considerate	Controlled
5	Refreshing	Resourceful	Respectful	Reserved
6	Spirited	Self-reliant	Sensitive	Satisfied
7	Promoter	Positive	Planner	Patient
8	Spontaneous	Sure	Scheduled	Shy
9	Optimistic	Outspoken	Orderly	Obliging
10	Funny	Forceful	Faithful	Friendly
11	Delightful	Daring	Detailed	Diplomatic
12	Cheerful	Confident	Cultured	Consistent
13	Inspiring	Independent	Idealistic	Inoffensive
14	Demonstrative	Decisive	Deep	Dry humor
15	Mixes easily	Mover	Musical	Mediator
16	Talker	Tenacious	Thoughtful	Tolerant
17	Lively	Leader	Loyal	Listener
18	Cute	Chief	Chartmaker	Contented
19	Popular	Productive	Perfectionist	Pleasant
20	Bouncy	Bold	Behaved	Balanced

TOTALS _____

WEAKNESSES

	SANGUINE POPULAR	CHOLERIC POWERFUL	MELANCHOLY PERFECT	PHLEGMATIC PEACEFUL
21	Brassy	Bossy	Bashful	Blank
22	Undisciplined	Unsympathetic	Unforgiving	Unenthusiastic
23	Repetitious	Resistant	Resentful	Reticent
24	Forgetful	Frank	Fussy	Fearful
25	Interrupts	Impatient	Insecure	Indecisive
26	Unpredictable	Unaffectionate	Unpopular	Uninvolved
27	Haphazard	Headstrong	Hard-to-please	Hesitant
28	Permissive	Proud	Pessimistic	Plain
29	Angered easily	Argumentative	Alienated	Aimless
30	Naive	Nervy	Negative attitude	Nonchalant
31	Wants credit	Workaholic	Withdrawn	Worrier
32	Talkative	Tactless	Too sensitive	Timid
33	Disorganized	Domineering	Depressed	Doubtful
34	Inconsistent	Intolerant	Introvert	Indifferent
35	Messy	Manipulative	Moody	Mumbles
36	Show-off	Stubborn	Skeptical	Slow
37	Loud	Lord-over-others	Loner	Lazy
38	Scatterbrained	Short tempered	Suspicious	Sluggish
39	Restless	Rash	Revengeful	Reluctant
40	Changeable	Crafty	Critical	Compromising
TOTALS				
COMBINED TOTALS				

Questions to Ask Yourself

Take the "Personality Profile." What is your temperament combination? (Indicated by the two highest totals.)

Look over the strengths and weaknesses for your temperament combination and list those which best describe you.

Make a list of the occupations and activities in which your particular temperament combination would be best.

Try to observe the temperament makeup of your closest family members and those with whom you work. List ways your temperament complements theirs and ways their temperaments challenge yours.

10

Launching Out Spirituality

Getting to know your spiritual strengths and abilities is a key part of the launching out process. The more we know about ourselves, the better equipped we are to take those first steps in getting on with our lives.

Recently our pastor, Dr. Larry Poland, helped the people in our church discover our motivational gifts. Others have often told me that I have the gift of serving. I thought so too, until the pastor remarked, "The person who has the gift of serving will much rather help with the serving of a banquet than to sit at the head table."

I thought, *That's not me. No way. Leave that kind of work to someone else.* Now if I see a person crying in a corner, I am glad to go talk with him, help him, serve in that way, yes. But waiting tables, scrubbing floors, doing dishes—no thank you. I can do those things well, but they wouldn't be my first choice of things to do.

My mother truly has the gift of serving. At my parents' fiftieth anniversary party, my mom said, "Honey, if you could just greet the people at the door and I could work in the kitchen, we'd get along fine."

When I took the motivational gifts test Dr. Poland

108

wrote, my strengths were exhibited in the gift of declaration and the gift of encouragement, which I think I had confused with the gift of serving. This test has greatly helped me to know myself.

Below I've listed the attributes of my motivational gifts as indicated by Dr. Poland's test:

- I have great difficulty handling situations in which moral evil is overlooked or treated lightly.
- I have a deep desire to identify and define righteousness and to confront evil.
- I have a strong tendency to see moral issues as clearly right or wrong with no gradations or "shades of gray."
- I often have a deeply felt need to proclaim to others my inner convictions about right and wrong.
- When I share my convictions publicly, people often respond as if I have God's authority, and they are convicted in their hearts by what I share.
- I tend to rely deeply on scriptural authority when I speak and may even communicate an attitude of "Thus says the Lord."
- It is common for others to share their innermost secrets or heartaches with me and, after sharing, to leave comforted, encouraged and able to "go forward."
- I have an ability to translate biblical truth into practical, real-life applications in such a way that people's lives are greatly changed by it.
- I find myself consistently being an "advisor" or "counselor" to others and am annoyed when my counsel is not applied.
- I have a deep, inner desire to encourage and build others through communicating the content and principles of God's Word.
- I am reluctant to communicate information or truth to others that may have a negative or demotivational effect on them.

Knowing my motivational gifts has greatly enhanced the ministry I have with others because I am able to use my gifts to their potential. Dr. Poland bases his test (which is included on the following pages) on the gifts listed in Romans 12. While other gifts are listed in different places in the New Testament, those listed in Romans 12 are generally considered the gifts that allow us to minister to others.

If you do not accumulate the suggested 30-35 points in any area, don't be discouraged — there could be several explanations. If you are a new Christian, your gift may not be fully developed at this point. Also, if you have been raised in a dysfunctional family or have experienced abuse or severe trauma, the test could be distorted because of the pain in your life. As those issues are resolved, you will more than likely see your gift (or gifts) emerge.

Motivational Gifts Inventory*

The following is an inventory to help you identify your own motivational gifts given by the Holy Spirit for the building up of the Body of Christ.

Instructions

Read carefully and thoughtfully the description of each facet of the gift and enter a number (1 to 5) in the blank on the left that reflects your response:

5 = "That **definitely** describes me!"

4 = "That **may well** describe me."

3 = "That **may** or **may not** describe me."

2 = "That **doesn't sound much** like me."

1 = "That **definitely isn't** me!"

---

* © 1987, Larry W. Poland. Reprinted with permission.

After entering numbers in each of the seven blanks for a motivation, total the numbers in those seven blanks. Your total will indicate the following:

30-35 points = You **most likely** possess that gift.

24-29 points = You **may well** possess that gift.

17-23 points = It is **difficult to determine** whether you possess that motivation.

11-16 points = You **probably do not** have that gift.

5-10 points = You **most likely do not** possess that gift.

Teaching

_____ 1. I get deep enjoyment from the study of God's Word even for long hours and with much effort.

_____ 2. I tend to be quite thorough in both the study and presentation of God's Word.

_____ 3. I have a deep, inner motivation to know the "whole truth" coupled with a deep desire to explain it to others.

_____ 4. I am annoyed by teaching that I feel is based on superficial research or is inaccurate or inconsistent in the use of biblical words.

_____ 5. I realize that I tend to test the level of knowledge of those teaching me God's Word.

_____ 6. I have an ability to explain complicated concepts in such a way that people understand and benefit from biblical truth.

_____ 7. I make a consistent effort to improve my teaching method and content to enable people to understand even more clearly what is taught.

_____ **Total**

Prophecy/Declaration

_____ 1. I have a deep desire to identify and define righteousness and to confront evil.

_____ 2. I have a strong tendency to see moral issues as clearly right or wrong with no gradations or "shades of gray."

_____ 3. I often have a deeply felt need to proclaim to others my inner convictions about right and wrong.

_____ 4. When I share my convictions publicly, people often respond as if I have God's authority, and they are convicted in their hearts by what I share.

_____ 5. I have great difficulty handling situations in which moral evil is overlooked or treated lightly.

_____ 6. I am willing to take stands publicly that may be both strong and controversial.

_____ 7. I tend to rely deeply on scriptural authority when I speak and may even communicate an attitude of "Thus says the Lord."

_____ **Total**

Exhortation/Encouragement

_____ 1. I have a deep, inner desire to encourage and build others through communicating the content and principles of God's Word.

_____ 2. I am reluctant to communicate information or truth to others that may have a negative or demotivational effect on them.

_____ 3. It is common for others to share their innermost secrets or heartaches with me and, after sharing, to leave comforted, encouraged and able to "go forward."

_____ 4. I have an ability to translate biblical truth into practical, real-life applications in such a way that people's lives are greatly changed by it.

_____ 5. I find myself rather consistently being an "advisor" or "counselor" to others and am annoyed when my counsel is not applied.

_____ 6. I get frustrated with teaching or truth that appears to be "impractical" or not easily translatable into Christian growth and upbuilding.

_____ 7. I have an ability to visualize a specific goal and to communicate it to others in a way in which they are eager and willing to pursue it.

_____ **Total**

Serving/Helps

_____ 1. I have a deep, inner desire to help other people by meeting their practical needs.

_____ 2. I seem to have an almost "intuitive" perception of the needs of others and immediately respond to reach out in a practical way to meet them.

_____ 3. I seem to have a virtually "tireless" ability to serve others, not only without complaining but also with great joy.

_____ 4. I am willing to do tasks that others probably consider "menial" with no other thought of how the service might appear to others.

_____ 5. I tend to meet the practical or concrete needs of others rather than discern their more abstract needs.

_____ 6. I delight in serving, even if I don't get any recognition.

_____ 7. I delight in doing tasks that enable leadership to be more effective.

_____ **Total**

Giving

_____ 1. I have a sensitivity to recognize the material needs of others and God's work.

_____ 2. I have a deep desire to give whatever I have to meet the material needs of others with little or no regard for the consequences to myself.

_____ 3. I derive great enjoyment from meeting the material needs of others in an anonymous manner, drawing no attention to myself or the gift.

_____ 4. I am careful in the way I handle my personal finances and have a pattern of success — almost an "instinct" for acquiring wealth.

_____ 5. I have a deep conviction that all I own belongs to God, and I think I live out this conviction in regard to money and material things.

_____ 6. I tend to view money just as a means to do the work of God and not of any value in and of itself.

_____ 7. I like to give as a challenge to others to give.

_____ **Total**

Mercy

_____ 1. I have an ability to empathize and sympathize in such a way that others know I care and hurt for them.

_____ 2. I delight in ministering to the needs of those who are hurting.

_____ 3. I delight in sharing time, talent and treasure without restraint with those who are helpless, downtrodden and exploited.

_____ 4. I seem to be able to "read" when others are hurting, even when there are few, if any, outward signs.

_____ 5. I have an ability to show mercy to hurting people without personally losing a cheerful spirit.

_____ 6. I ache internally and often weep when I learn of others who hurt, even if they are not personal acquaintances or friends.

_____ 7. Because of my personal sensitivity to others, I often feel that those who do not respond the way I do to suffering are "callous" or "harsh."

_____ **Total**

Ruling/Administration

_____ 1. I have a deep, inner motivation to see things done in an orderly, efficient manner and feel uneasy or get frustrated when they are not.

_____ 2. I greatly enjoy taking on a management "mess," sorting it out, structuring it, and getting it to work smoothly.

_____ 3. I have a tendency to assume responsibility for organizing things if no structured leadership to do so exists.

_____ 4. I have an almost intuitive feel for the kinds of details that others tend to overlook when they manage and an ability to examine a plan in terms of what it will take to execute the details of it.

_____ 5. I have a desire to see tasks completed as quickly as possible and a need to have tasks that have foreseeable terminations to them. I dislike tasks that "never end" or that are long term.

_____ 6. I tend to be quite objective and fair in my approach to the ingredients and perspectives that are part of a solution. I am not influenced much by feelings or personal desires when administering.

_____ 7. I am willing to carry out the details of plans that are created by others.

_____ **Total**

Faith

_____ 1. I am consistently able to trust God in both little and big matters.

_____ 2. I have an ability to operate with little or no visible resources and maintain an abiding confidence that God will provide them when needed.

_____ 3. I have an ability to visualize clearly the work that God will do and to thank Him sincerely for it before it can be seen with the eyes of sight.

_____ 4. I have a consistent attitude of expectation that God is working and will work, even when there is no confirming evidence to support the expectation and there are significant obstacles in view.

_____ 5. I have the belief that God will "work a miracle" even in situations in which there is no known precedent for God's miraculous work.

_____ 6. I have a strong desire to motivate others to have implicit faith in God.

_____ 7. I am able to keep my faith unshaken even in situations in which a miracle is not forthcoming and a solution is not as I had visualized.

_____ **Total**

Summary

Look back over the totals for each gift and enter the scores in rank order as indicated below.

	Gift	**Points**
My **highest** score was:	_____	_____
My **next highest** score:	_____	_____

Next: _____   _____

Next: _____   _____

Next: _____   _____

Next: _____   _____

Next to lowest   _____   _____

My **lowest** score: _____   _____

Place a star beside those gifts which scored more than 30 points. These are most likely your gifts. Gifts which scored more than 24 but less than 30 points may well be secondary motivations.

Note: This inventory is not precise enough to enable you to draw conclusions based on score differences of less than three points. Therefore, it would be wise to "group" the highest and lowest gifts (your three highest scores and your three lowest scores). If your scores were all rather low (all less than thirty), look for those gifts or "groups" of gifts that are separated by at least four points from the other gifts on the high and low end.

Whether you are starting over in a business or a marriage, staying home and working with your family, trying to discover what you want to do now, or looking for your nitch as a new Christian, the understanding of your personalities and spiritual gifts will greatly help you. I encourage you to take the temperament inventory, the spiritual gifts inventory, and avail yourself of colleges that offer personality tests and skill tests. Recovering from a broken dream puts you at a crossroads in your life. Take time to prepare yourself in every way possible to know yourself better and to enable yourself to make wise decisions for your future.

Questions to Ask Yourself

What are your spiritual gifts?

List some of the attributes of your particular gifts.

Make a list of the ways you can exercise your spiritual gifts in your home, in your church, and in your work.

11

Launching Out With Compassion

A year ago I was assisting in a C.L.A.S.S. (Christian Leaders, Artists and Speakers Seminars) as a group leader. During these three-day seminars, we divide into small groups, assigning one leader to every ten conferees.

I was the one responsible for putting people into groups. Since I knew nothing about the people at the seminar, I just prayed, "Lord, please help me employ my organizational system and then use that system to get each person into the right group."

I ended up with seven women and three men in my group. In my experiences as a group leader, I have found that women are generally more open about themselves than men. I was desirous for the entire group, including the men, to share something of their heart and life rather than just their personal accomplishments and credentials.

I prayed, "Lord, open the men up. Help them to share themselves rather than just be content to let the women share personal experiences. Don't let it scare them if the women share. Let it move them emotionally and spiritually."

Showing Compassion Isn't Always Easy

I got into my group that afternoon and proceeded in my normal fashion. In the first session we have each person introduce himself or herself to the group. I usually ask, "Who would like to be first?" because I don't like to put people on the spot.

While the group prepared for their three-minute introductions, I felt the Lord say to me, *Start with the lady on your right.*

I don't do that, Lord, I hastily replied. *You know I don't like to put people on the spot. What if she says, "No, I don't want to do it yet"?*

I kept hearing the Lord say, *Start with the lady on your right.*

So I very timidly asked, "Would you like to be first?"

She eagerly said, "Yes, I'd like to."

When she started to speak, she began to cry. She looked at me and said, "I knew I was going to be in your group, and I told the Lord I didn't want to be here."

I thought, *I wonder what's going on? Maybe she's lost a child, but why wouldn't she want to be in my group?*

She continued, "My son was in a car accident last December. His fianceé was killed. My son was a drunk driver."

Immediately my heart and my head were battling harsh feelings: *If I'd known about that, I wouldn't have put you in my group. I would've given you to someone else.*

She started talking about how difficult her situation was. Her son was facing a seven-month jail term.

I was thinking, *Only seven months? Why didn't he get seven years?*

Then the Lord spoke to me, *Marilyn, I want you to*

comfort this lady.

I looked at her as she was sobbing and talking about all the difficult things she was facing. Normally I'd be hugging and comforting someone going through pain like that. But this time I thought, *No, I can't do that. I think her son ought to go to jail. I don't really feel too sorry for her.*

The Lord began to do a work in me right there. He said, *Marilyn, you said you've forgiven the drunk driver. You've said you trusted Me in this situation. Trust Me with this lady and show compassion to her.*

I finally stood up and walked over to her in faith. I had no idea what I was going to say. I didn't know if I could get anything out. I looked at her and said, "As a mother of a son who was killed by a drunk driver, I want you to know that I love you." I then hugged her. The woman just sobbed and sobbed and fell into my arms. As I looked around at the group, I realized there wouldn't be a problem with the men opening up. They weren't just shedding tears; they were sobbing. I have never had a group open up as that group did.

As we got around to the last lady in the group, she stood up and said, "I knew God was going to put me in your group, and I wanted to be here. I'm from Carrollton, Kentucky. I have just been working with the families of the twenty-seven people who were killed in the bus fire caused by a drunk driver. I have been doing everything I can to see to it that the drunk driver stayed in jail for the rest of his life. Today God has shown me that there are two sides to every story."

She walked over to the lady whose son was a drunk driver and they hugged each other tightly. When we were finished, I walked out of that room and Florence Littauer looked at me and said, "Are you all right?"

I replied, "No."

She said, "Do you want to talk about it?"

"No!"

I ran to my room and cried, "Lord, that wasn't fair. You put me in such a difficult position. It wasn't easy to show compassion to that mother."

God gently replied, *Marilyn, you had a rough edge which needed to be smoothed off. You need to have compassion for a lady like this. She is one of My children, too, and she's hurting right now.*

Allow God to Use You

The next day, the lady came to the group and said, "I need to speak first and I need to talk about my son again. I know this is hard on you, but will you please let me talk?"

I nodded, and she said, "I want you to know my husband and I are born-again Christians. We raised our children in a Christian home. We don't understand what happened. Ever since my son's accident, I have thought somehow it must be my fault."

Her words struck a familiar chord. She was just like the rest of us. She was a victim, too.

She continued, "I have been thinking, 'I need somebody to forgive me, somebody to love me.' Yesterday you did and you released me."

Patsy Clairmont, a fellow member of the C.L.A.S.S. staff, is writing a book titled *God Uses Cracked Pots*. She shares that we are earthen vessels and the cracks in our life come from the pain we go through. She points out that Jesus' light is able to shine through us because it shines through the cracks. As we show compassion to other hurting people, some of our own pain is eased, but we will always have the scars. If we are willing, though, those scars can be turned into usable cracks allowing God's light to shine through to a needy world.

I guess I'm a cracked pot, too. There are many cracks in my life, but I pray that the light of compassion, the light of love, the light of just bowing before the Lord Jesus and saying, "God, I don't understand it, but use it," can shine through me. I pray that each of you will allow God to work through you. Rather than being bitter because my dreams have died and people have hurt me, I'm going to work at being better. I'm going to launch out with God's compassion.

Questions to Ask Yourself

Write down an opportunity you had this past week to show compassion to someone.

How did you do? Did you respond to the need? If not, why not?

Ask God to show you what there is in your life or personality which keeps you from showing compassion. Write down what God shows you.

Name one thing you are going to do this week to show compassion to someone else who has experienced pain similar to yours.

Living
Again

I've dreamed many dreams that never came true
I've seen them vanish at dawn,
But I've realized enough of my dreams, thank God
To make me want to dream on.

I've prayed many prayers when no answer came,
Though I waited patient and long;
But answers have come to enough of my prayers
To make me keep praying on.

I've trusted many a friend who failed
And left me to weep alone;
But I've found enough of my friends true blue
To make me keep trusting on.

I've sown many seed that fell by the way
For the birds to feed upon,
But I've held enough golden sheaves in my hands
To make me keep sowing on.

I've drained the cup of disappointment and pain
And gone many days without song;
But I've sipped enough nectar from the roses of life
To make me want to live on.

— Author Unknown

12

Living Again
With New Dreams

I first heard the poem on the previous page at the Compassionate Friends National Convention in Tampa, Florida. It was read by Calvin Ijames in memory of his son Jeff.

I imagine every person reading this book can identify with the feelings of the poem. We have all experienced unfulfilled dreams, seemingly unanswered prayers, unfaithful friends, unfruitful seeds, and unhappy days. But enough dreams have been fulfilled, enough prayers have been answered, enough friends have been faithful, enough seeds have been fruitful, and enough days have been happy to make us want to live on. Our perspective and expectations may have changed, but it is possible to face life after the death of a dream with more strength and determination than we ever had before.

In an article titled "Dreams: Pathway to Potential," Kent Hutcheson writes:

> A person who has dreams is filled with expectation, and no obstacle seems insurmountable. He has a positive attitude, is excited and is never bored.
>
> A person without dreams is characterized by a

sense of duty and obligation. He does things because "I have to do this," or "I will get into trouble (or people won't like me) if I don't," rather than doing things from a sense of inner motivation.[1]

Mr. Hutcheson gives three secrets to forming a specific dream worth capturing: (1) Have the necessary mindset; (2) pray 'Lord Jesus, If You were I, what would you do?'; and (3) mentally acknowledge God's control over your life and, consequently, over the dream He has given to you.[2] He also shares what can kill a dream: "Timidity or unbelief, a sense of inadequacy, fear of failure, avoiding risk, and pursuing your own dreams instead of God's."[3]

A passage of scripture which always encourages me to live again with new dreams is found in Hebrews 11. It is often referred to as God's "Hall of Fame":

> What is faith? It is the confident assurance that something we want is going to happen. It is the certainty that what we hope for is waiting for us, even though we cannot see it up ahead. Men of God in days of old were famous for their faith.
>
> By faith—by believing God—we know that the world and the stars—in fact, all things—were made at God's command; and that they were all made from things that can't be seen.

When my faith is wavering, it is encouraging to me to remind myself that the God to whom I am praying is the God who created the world and stars. He made all things. If He is the controller of the entire universe, sure He can control my situation.

> It was by faith that Abel obeyed God and brought an offering that pleased God more than Cain's offering did. God accepted Abel and proved it by accepting his gift; and though Abel is long dead, we can still learn lessons from him about trusting God.

Enoch trusted God too, and that is why God took him away to heaven without dying; suddenly he was gone because God took him. Before this happened God had said how pleased he was with Enoch. You can never please God without faith, without depending on him. Anyone who wants to come to God must believe that there is a God and that he rewards those who sincerely look for him.

Noah was another who trusted God. When he heard God's warning about the future, Noah believed him even though there was then no sign of a flood, and wasting no time, he built the ark and saved his family. Noah's belief in God was in direct contrast to the sin and disbelief of the rest of the world—which refused to obey—and because of his faith he became one of those whom God has accepted.

Noah is always an encouragement to me when I am trying to hold on to my faith. Surely my situation is much simpler than his. God hasn't asked me to prepare for a flood when we've never had rain. He hasn't asked me to become the laughingstock of my community. If Noah could remain faithful through his troubles, I can hang on to my faith in the midst of my problems.

Oswald Chambers writes, "Faith in God is a terrific venture in the dark; I have to believe that God is good in spite of all that contradicts it in my experience."[4]

Abraham trusted God, and when God told him to leave home and go far away to another land which he promised to give him, Abraham obeyed. Away he went, not even knowing where he was going. And even when he reached God's promised land, he lived in tents like a mere visitor, as did Isaac and Jacob, to whom God gave the same promise. Abraham did this because he was confidently waiting for God to bring him to that strong heavenly city whose designer and builder is God.

Sarah, too, had faith, and because of this she was

able to become a mother in spite of her old age, for she realized that God, who gave her his promise, would certainly do what he said. And so a whole nation came from Abraham, who was too old to have even one child—a nation with so many millions of people that, like the stars of the sky and the sand on the ocean shores, there is no way to count them.

These men of faith I have mentioned died without ever receiving all that God had promised them; but they saw it all awaiting them on ahead and were glad, for they agreed that this earth was not their real home but that they were just strangers visiting down here. And quite obviously when they talked like that, they were looking forward to their real home in heaven.

If they had wanted to, they could have gone back to the good things of this world. But they didn't want to. They were living for heaven. And now God is not ashamed to be called their God, for he has made a heavenly city for them (Hebrews 11:1-16, TLB).

Those of us who have faith in God, those who have watched dreams die but are determined to live and dream again, can be included in God's Hall of Fame.

I met Jeremy at my favorite department store where he is a salesman. I commented I was working on a book and Jeremy became quite interested, especially when I mentioned the title *When Your Dreams Die.*

"Oh, I can identify with that title," he volunteered.

Jeremy and his wife were married less than a year when their first child was born prematurely at twenty-seven weeks. She lived only ten days. Within six months Jeremy and his wife separated. In one year they experienced the death of their child and the death of their marriage.

Jeremy realized he could do nothing about their child, but he believed their marriage could be resurrected.

He and his former wife cautiously started dating again. Now they are planning to remarry. Both have matured. Both have learned more about themselves. Both have worked on building a relationship that will last. Their dream has been altered, but it will live again.

New Dreams Out of Old

My friend Scott defines a dream as "the possible — what life *can* be." Scott felt comfortable in his family. There seemed to be wholeness for many generations before him. However, his security and dreams were shattered the day his parents told him they were getting a divorce. Scott was a young adult at the time, a mature Christian, a rational thinker. Yet, his reaction was typical of any child when parents decide to divorce: "It must be my fault. What did I do wrong? How can I fix this?"

The day his anger exploded at someone he loved dearly, Scott knew he had to find a friend with whom he could talk out his frustrations and fears. He now feels that through understanding his parents' past he is finding peace in his present. He has been able to absolve himself of any blame. He realizes he still has difficulty trusting others and he resists pursuing new relationships, but he continues to work on these areas.

Scott had no control over his parents' marriage or divorce, but he did have control over how he reacted. Once he received some wise counsel, he felt more comfortable in verbalizing his emotions before a volcano of anger built up inside him. Scott is a very talented young man. He has taken the emotions, sensitivity, and wisdom he has gained through his altered dreams and created plays and musicals that touch the hearts of audiences. He has made his pain work for him.

Sue shared earlier how her dream died when her

marriage ended. She says:

> I think of my life as a tapestry. Over the past few years I have had to spend time plucking out threads of dreams that don't fit anymore. Residue and impurities from old dreams can cover the picture on my tapestry. I reserve some threads and I rework others. Through counseling and talking with others, I have been able to face the pain, hurt and fears. I am learning to dream again.

Wayne, who lost his job, writes:

> Living again with a damaged dream was very hard to accept. Suddenly roles in our house were reversed – I was home and my wife went to work. But her job turned out to be a blessing in disguise. Many times when we were together the negative emotions of depression and fear would be magnified. When my wife was at work, I was all the more motivated to get started in my own job search.
>
> Living again without being in control was also difficult to do. As a Choleric, I love being in control. Yet I had to surrender *everything* to God – my career, my family, our future. I wasn't used to that, but my success depended on it.
>
> Living again also meant having to face the fact that I didn't have a job. Cholerics love to work. I had no "work" to do other than look for a job, and that gave me no sense of accomplishment. Before I had supervised people, been in charge, faced many challenges. Now I was reduced to being alone, supervising only myself, and my job-hunt challenge was surrounded by worry and guilt.
>
> But now, all of that is behind us. We're starting a new dream in a new city. Sure it was hard to start over, but God has opened a great window of opportunity for us. He has given me a fine job that is almost a perfect match for my strengths. He is returning our sense of security and showing us the tools we need to minister to others. We are truly living again.

Building New Dreams

Learning to dream again will come very slowly for many of you. It did for me. It took a long time before I allowed myself even to consider there could be life outside of my original dream. Building new dreams is hard work.

My new dream was that God would use my experiences in a significant way to glorify Himself and to honor my sons. God was willing to do that, but it took my cooperation and my willingness to be vulnerable. I had to be willing to admit how much I hurt, how Glen and I struggled as we grieved differently, and how I wrestled with God's plan for my life.

Evaluate Your Skills

I knew I had a story to tell that others needed to hear. I knew my spiritual gifts were exhortation and encouragement, and my temperament was Choleric/Melancholy. This information told me I had abilities that would be beneficial for a speaker.

Get Ready

Knowing all of this, however, did not make me a speaker. First, I needed training in how to speak and present my story effectively. I attended C.L.A.S.S. (Christian Leaders, Artists and Speakers Seminars) and the speakers training for M.A.D.D. (Mothers Against Drunk Driving).

Be Available

I had to be willing to use my training and abilities and then practice, practice, practice. I accepted nearly every invitation to speak which was extended to me. I spoke to groups of five or six people and to groups of several hundred. My dream of being able to use my story to help and encourage others began to come true.

Living Again

In all honesty, the mother side of me would still like to simply be the mom of five healthy, normal children. But the child of God side of me stands in awe at God's plan and His creativity in using me and helping me discover talents and abilities I didn't know I had.

My friend Helen shared with me her thoughts on learning to live with new dreams in spite of multiple sclerosis:

> I look back and think how thrilled I was to be in the Air Force Band and play for President Kennedy's inauguration. I think about the wonderful satisfaction I had in teaching, directing, and shaping a group of multiethnic inner city kids into an orchestra that played Mozart so beautifully it almost broke your heart.
>
> But I can tell you, that is *nothing* compared to the thrill of getting a letter from someone half a world away telling me how learning about Jesus from braille Scriptures in his language has changed his life. I know now that God's plan for each of us is always so much better than anything we can ever imagine for ourselves.
>
> I will probably never be completely well. I tire easily, put up with incontinence, have a very awkward gait because I lack sensation in my legs, and have embarrassing falls in public.
>
> But the Lord has been extremely good to me. I have heard of so many MS sufferers who are bedridden or bound to a wheelchair. I am able to walk, and am continually being challenged.
>
> Even though I can no longer teach full time or play an instrument, God has not let my former skills go to waste. For a couple of years I taught a beginning instrument class several hours each week at a local Christian school. Singing in the church choir and in small ensembles has provided a wonderful outlet. I'm even using the three years of French I took in high school. I've em-

bossed the entire New Testament in French braille on printing plates and I translate all the letters in French that come to the LBW home office.

One of the things I am most grateful for is that I was allowed so many more years with my wonderful, supportive husband, and that I *did* get to see my children grow up. My son has graduated from college and is now in his first year at seminary. My daughter is a senior in college and is planning to be a Christian counselor. The blessings never cease.

I am convinced that whether your time on this earth is long or short, full of happiness or pain, ease or hardship, gain or loss, the Lord can use your life to His glory. His power is shown in how He uses you in your weakness, and living to glorify Him can bring you more happiness than following any dream you may have ever had.

I recently saw a quote on a piece of stationery which said, "The poorest of all men is not the man without a cent but the man without a dream."

I challenge you to let go of the old destroyed and damaged dreams, launch out to available opportunities, and live again with your new, God-given dreams.

13

Living Again With Confidence

Recently my little three-year-old friend Crystal was visiting me. We were watching *The Wizard of Oz* and Crystal was enjoying it until the Wicked Witch of the West appeared. Crystal said, "I don't think I like that lady."

I tried to assure her that the whole story was make-believe and there was nothing to be afraid of. But in a few minutes my little friend asked, "Is that grumpy old lady going to be on again?"

I said, "She will be on some more, but since we are watching this on the VCR, we don't have to see those parts. We can fast forward her right out of the picture!"

Crystal was satisfied. She sat back, relaxed and enjoyed the good parts of the story. Each time the "grumpy old lady" tried to make an appearance, we just zapped her right off the screen.

Wouldn't it be wonderful if we could do that in real life? Whenever something scary, painful or unhappy started to enter our lives, we could press the fast forward button and zap those situations away. Unfortunately, the fast forward button doesn't work in real life. Most of you reading this book have already had plenty of scary, painful and unhappy situations in your lives, and there are no guarantees there won't be more.

However, because you have come through these difficult situations, you can be better prepared for any future crises in your life. You have survived. You are on your way to recovery. You know yourself better than you did before.

If you have followed the suggestions in this book, you are learning to trust yourself and others. You are discovering more about yourself every day. You know your God-given temperament and your spiritual gifts. You now have some ideas where you fit into the scheme of life again. It is my prayer that you also know God better than you did before. Hopefully, you have started on a program of journalizing your thoughts and writing your prayers daily.

You're ready to try living again.

Nervous, but ready.

In this book we've covered the process of

Letting   **Go**
Launching   **Out**
Living   **Again**

Notice that when you remove the words beginning with L, you are left with a command: Go Out Again. I believe that is what God is saying to you and me today: *Don't be afraid. Gather up everything you have learned. Get it organized in your mind and incorporated into your lifestyle. Go out again.*

Although I can't guarantee you a worry-free life, I can give you some tips on being prepared to face life with confidence — traumas and all.

Rely on God's Word

We will be much better prepared for the traumas and the trials in our lives if we maintain a constant two-way communication with God. The midst of a trial is not a good time to have to "catch up" with God. If you are steeped in God's Word and solid in your relationship with Him, you will be able to draw on the resources of His power, His peace and His protection immediately when troubles come.

When our little grandchild Kate was wavering between life and death, I did not have to take time to get reacquainted with God. We were already on speaking terms. We were such good friends that I could even say, "You have hurt me. You have thrown me a curve. Please give me some words that will comfort me and let me know You're still on my side." Our relationship was strong enough that I could be completely honest with God. I was surprised at His actions, but I didn't doubt his God-hood, His deity, His sovereignty. My confidence in Him as Lord of all remained steadfast.

Restore Relationships

Through the death of our first two sons, we learned about the fragility of life. We realized that when we tucked a child into bed at night, we had no guarantee he would be alive in the morning.

We adopted a "Prayed-up, Loved-up, Confessed-up" policy in our home. We wanted to always be prayed-up about all of the important issues in our lives and in our family. We didn't want to say with regret, "If only we had prayed about it more. Perhaps things would be different."

We were loved-up. As the kids left for school in the morning, I always tried to call out one last "I love you" as they walked out the door. Since Nathan's death, I am even more generous with "I love you." I seldom hang up from a telephone conversation with a family member or a close friend without a quick "I love you."

There is nothing as important as keeping "confessed-up." As you read this, if someone comes to mind with whom you are at odds, do something about it now. I realize relationships cannot be restored unless both parties agree, but be sure you have done your part. Many people are unable to resolve their grief over the death of a loved one because something was left unresolved in their relationship. Don't let that happen to you. Sometimes people have been hurt so deeply that a relationship will never be completely restored, and that is understandable. But do what you can to at least be on speaking terms with that person. Keep the doors open for future restoration of the relationship.

When we refuse to mend relationships, especially in our families, we not only hurt ourselves, but we also deprive our children from knowing about those who could be significant contributors to their lives. Children gain security by knowing of their ancestral origins, even if the family tree has produced a few bad apples.

Recognize God's Special Touch

It is true that God "sends rain on the just and on the unjust" (Matthew 5:45, TLB). No one in this world is exempt from pain and suffering, but we can choose how we will react to the bad that comes into our lives. As Christians we can be confident God is aware of our plight and He stands available to walk through our trials. We can choose to look for His special touch or we can choose to muddle though it alone.

Many times, when I was in the depths of despair, God reached out and touched me in a special way to assure me of His presence and His concern for me. I'd like to share a few of those experiences with you.

After Nathan's death, one of the stumbling blocks in my healing process was that I didn't have an opportunity for a final goodbye. I remember saying to God, "I'm not going to argue with You about You allowing Nathan to die. He belonged to You before he belonged to me, and I respect Your sovereignty. However, couldn't You have at least caused the hospital to allow me to see him before he died or even in the first moments after his death? Surely a sovereign God could have arranged that."

Within a few weeks of Nate's death I had a dream — a very, very real dream. Nate was standing at the foot of my bed. He was wearing the clothes he had on the night he died. As I reached for him, he stepped back out of my reach, but he smiled and waved goodbye. Then he was gone. God gave me my own private opportunity to say goodbye to my son. That stumbling block was removed. One of God's special touches. His response to a grieving mother's need.

God has reached out to me in many other ways as well. I dreaded the first Christmas after Nate's death, especially because Christmas Day was Nate's birthday. I had told some friends I would like to cancel December and try it again some other year. Soon after I had made that statement, I found a poster which said, "God gives us memories so we might have roses in December."[1]

God has consistently given beautiful December roses in the seven years since Nate's death. Living without Nate has been very difficult, but with each special rose God has given me the assurance that He is aware of my pain, He hurts with me, and with His strength I can even enjoy living again.

When we were at the cemetery for Nathan's burial, there were several news reporters and photographers in attendance and frequently their cameras were fixed on Glen and me, the grieving parents. I knew the kind of picture they were looking for—a sobbing mother in the arms of a distraught father. I was not ashamed of our tears, but I really didn't want that picture embedded forever in the minds of those who knew Nate. I was so determined that the photographers would not get such a picture that I smiled at them each time their cameras were focused on us.

One photographer was equally determined. As Glen and I walked toward the funeral director's car, the photographer was ready with his camera. As we approached the photographer, our pastor led those at the funeral in singing the chorus *Because He Lives.* Glen and I squeezed each other's hand tightly and sang with all the strength we had:

> Because He lives I can face tomorrow.
> Because He lives all fear is gone.
> Because I know He holds the future,
> My life is worth the living.
> Just because He lives.[2]

The photographer's eyes filled with tears. The camera slid to his side and he never took the picture.

Each time I hear that beautiful little chorus, I am reminded of God's faithfulness and of the basis of my hope for life here and in the hereafter. Because He lives I can face tomorrow. So can you.

Your dreams have died or been altered. Life has not turned out exactly the way you planned. You are coming to terms with your vulnerability and the fragility of life. You don't know the future and neither do I, but God does. As you spend time getting to know the author of the future, He will give you the confidence to *GO OUT AGAIN.*

Notes

Chapter One

1. Found on a bookmark by Sunshine Thoughts, Antioch Publishing Company, Yellow Springs, Ohio 45387.

2. Melody Beattie, *Codependent No More* (New York: Harper/Hazeldon, 1987), p. 118.

3. Marion Bond West, "An Unsuspected Friend," *Guideposts* (September 1989), pp. 6-9.

Chapter Four

1. Lewis B. Smedes, *Forgive and Forget* (San Francisco: Harper and Row Publishers, 1984), p. 39.

2. Janice Harris Lord is the author of *No Time for Goodbyes* and *Beyond Sympathy,* published by Pathfinder Publishing, Ventura, California.

3. Smedes, p. 5.

4. Lewis B. Smedes, "Forgiveness: Healing the Hurts We Don't Deserve," *Family Life Today* (January 1985), pp. 24-28.

4. Jan Frank, *A Door of Hope* (San Bernardino: Here's Life Publishers, 1987), p. 28.

6. Stormie Omartian, PTL television program, September 9, 1987.

7. Oswald Chambers, *The Best From All His Books,* Harry Verploegh, ed. (Nashville: Oliver-Nelson Publishers, 1987), p. 343.

8. Smedes, p. 133.

Chapter Five

1. A. B. Simpson and R. Kelso Carter, "Launch Out," *Inspiring Hymns,* compiled by Alfred B. Smith (Grand Rapids: Singspiration, Inc./Zondervan Publishing House, 1951).

Chapter Six

1. Oswald Chambers, *The Best From All His Books,* Harry Verploegh, ed. (Nashville: Oliver-Nelson Publishers, 1987), p. 363.

2. Chambers, p. 363.

3. Dick Purnell, *Knowing God By His Names* (San Bernardino: Here's Life Publishers, 1987).

Chapter Seven

1. Oswald Chambers, *The Best From All His Books,* Harry Verploegh,

ed. (Nashville: Oliver-Nelson Publishers, 1987), p. 246.

2. Chambers, 248.

Chapter Eight

1. *The Best of Florence Littauer,* compiled by Marilyn Willett Heavilin (San Bernardino: Here's Life Publishers, 1989), p. 139.

2. Marilyn Willett Heavilin, *Roses in December* (San Bernardino: Here's Life Publishers, 1986), pp. 71-72.

3. Oswald Chamber, *The Best From All His Books*, Harry Verploegh, ed. (Nashville: Oliver-Nelson Publishers, 1987) p. 366.

Chapter Nine

1. Lana Bateman, *Personality Patterns* (Dallas: Philippian Ministries, 1985).

2. Bateman, *Personality Patterns*.

3. Bateman, *Personality Patterns*.

4. Bateman, *Personality Patterns*.

Chapter Twelve

1. Kent Hutcheson, "Dreams: Pathway to Potential," *Worldwide Challenge* (May/June 1986), pp. 32-35.

2. Hutcheson, pp. 32-35.

3. Hutcheson, pp. 32-35.

4. Oswald Chambers, *The Best From All His Books,* Harry Verploegh, ed. (Nashville: Oliver-Nelson Publishers, 1987), p. 110.

Chapter Thirteen

1. This quote is generally credited to Sir James Barrie, the author of *Peter Pan*.

2. "Because He Lives." Words by William and Gloria Gaither. Music by William Gaither. © 1971, William Gaither. All rights reserved. Used by permission.